Urban Church Education

Contributors

Donald B. Rogers

Letty M. Russell

Chris Michael

Kay Kupper Berg

C. Renee Rust

Colleen Birchett

Robert E. Jones

Captolia D. Newbern

Lawrence L. Falk

William R. Myers

Bill Gambrell

Tom Boomershine

Terry Heck

Nellie Metz

Richard L. Stackpole

Ron Robotham

Urban Church Education

edited by
DONALD B. ROGERS

Religious Education Press
Birmingham, Alabama

Library of Congress Cataloging-in-Publication Data
Urban church education.
    Bibliography: p.
    Includes index.
    1. Christian education.   2. City churches.   I. Rogers, Donald B., 1931-
BV1471.2.U73 1989   268   89-4024
ISBN 0-89135-070-5

Religious Education Press, Inc.
5316 Meadow Brook Road
Birmingham, Alabama 35242
10 9 8 7 6 5 4 3 2

Religious Education Press publishes books exclusively in religious education and in areas closely related to religious education. It is committed to enhancing and professionalizing religious education through the publication of serious, significant, and scholarly works.

PUBLISHER TO THE PROFESSION

Contents

795.57

Acknowledgments

It is obvious that I have had much help in the creation of this book. Those who have contributed chapters have done so with a commitment to the urban church for which I am grateful.

I wish to thank others whose assistance is not as visible. The people of the school where I teach, United Theological Seminary in Dayton, Ohio, and of the church, Mt. Auburn Baptist in Cincinnati, Ohio, where I am pastor, have helped in important ways.

The office assistance of Brenda Paradiso greatly facilitated the preparation of the manuscript and the editing skills of Kay Kupper Berg greatly enhanced the quality of the writing. I am deeply indebted to them.

I also wish to thank Abingdon Press for granting permission to reprint in revised form the chapter by Letty Russell. The book would not have been possible without James Michael Lee's initiation of the project and his commitment to the publication of serious religious education books.

Chapter 1

Introduction and Overview

Donald B. Rogers

What is an urban church and why do we need to think in depth about the religious education work of urban churches?

Defining just what is and what is not an "urban church" is difficult because of the need to recognize the complexity and variety of such churches. Location is, of course, a key. Urban churches are churches in urban centers with population concentrations of 50,000 or more according to most government statistical records. The complexity arises when other factors are taken into consideration.

In my city there are churches that sit in rather self-contained and isolated neighborhoods. A significant percentage of the people in the neighborhood and the churches are recent arrivals from rural areas. The people return to their rural "homes" frequently to visit, for weddings and funerals and birthday parties and vacation times. The most successful social programs are those run with the assistance of the Appalachian Council. Are those churches urban in anything but address?

One of my seminary students has served the same church for over thirty years. It sits at a crossroad with a few houses in a rural neighborhood. Thirty years ago the congregation was mostly farm oriented. Then some rather well-to-do commuters arrived whose lives were focused on two very large metropolitan complexes. Later another group of people moved into the

1

neighborhood and the church. These were middle-income people living in new housing developments and commuting to smaller cities. In addition, a nearby small town has become a large town that is moving in and around the church building. To what extent has this church become a congregation in which urban realities are major factors and is thus "an urban church"?

Urban churches are those churches, usually in urban settings, that are heavily influenced by the realities of urban life because the people of the church work, live, and/or worship in ways affected by urban life. Some urban churches are urban neighborhood churches in that they have congregations and ministries that relate to the immediate geographic neighborhood where the church is located. Other urban churches are "specialized ministry" churches where a focus of ministry or a particular doctrinal emphasis or some other unique quality serves to bring together a congregation from a wider geographic urban area. Other urban churches are what I call "ground free" churches. These tend to be large churches that would seem to be what they are no matter where they are located. Such churches look much like each other whether they are downtown or in a suburb or out in the fields along a major interstate highway. They may or may not be conscious of an urban character.

The most perplexing urban church situations are those that are in the midst of transition caused by factors in urban life. These churches are often suffering financially and with a small base of available leadership. They may be churches that have seen a great change in their neighborhood. They may be churches that have become racial islands trying to achieve integration. They may be churches that find it difficult to get and keep well-qualified, full-time, professional leadership. But all urban churches have challenging situations in their education ministries.

The point of this book is that all urban churches face issues in their education ministries that are as complex as their total life and situation. These churches need to work more closely together, communicate more freely congregation to congregation, and become aggressively creative in resolving the issues of education ministry. The worldwide trends indicate that all nations are becoming urbanized and that the church in every land must solve the issues of ministry in urban settings or face great ineffectiveness.

This book about urban church education has grown out of my involvement in urban churches. Most of my years in the church have been spent in urban congregations. I grew up in one; I did field education in urban churches during my seminary days; I have served urban churches as religious educator and pastor in eight cities. I am the pastor of an urban congregation now, as well as a professor of religious education in a seminary that is committed to the education of pastors and educators for urban congregations.

In addition, an early influence on the direction for this book came from a survey of clergy alumni of my seminary which asked them to name important issues in urban church education. Over 250 clergy responded from 113 communities in 30 states. The range of their concerns was overwhelming. I had listed 41 topics that seemed to me to have some potential interest. The respondents added 45 others. (The complete list is in Appendix II.) The long list serves to indicate the complexity of the dimensions of education undertaken by the church in the urban setting.

In my first list the following were rated as being of high interest: ways to do community surveys / parochial school models / week-day released time schools / store-front schools / summer school options / tutoring programs / special remedial programs / alternatives in age-level grouping / skills information (storytelling, Bible study, memorization, lesson preparation) / busing / computer assisted education / and special issue needs (racism, feminism, peace education, ecology).

This book has been put together in general response to that interest indicator, with other factors taken into consideration. To a great extent I have sought out practitioners of urban religious education. I have done so in the belief that they are the people who have an essential credential for helping others: They are, or have been, directly involved in the issues. The authors represent a cross section of denominations and geography and experience.

In the pursuit of that sort of contribution I have discovered that many of those engaged in urban church education are reluctant to write about their work. Their reluctance seems to be based on their feeling that what they are doing is not significant enough to deserve close attention.

That understandable reticence reflects a sense of frustration that urban church educators have. Nothing works so well that those on the scene are not fully aware of limitations. I hope that this book helps us to step over that reluctance and begin to share more freely with each other whatever experience and insight we have. I have been disappointed that some who might have shared have chosen not to. As a result the book is not as complete as I had wished.

I feel that what urban religious educators need is encouragment, ideas, and examples that they can re-do for their own situation. There is much more to be shared, much more to be said, many more creative programs already in existence that need to be made known to others. To a critical degree, the challenges of urban church education are being met and will be resolved on the front lines by people who simply decide they have to do what needs to be done so that the church can fulfill in a better fashion the task of education.

Much of the attention given to the urban church came in the 1960s. That attention coincided with a new sense of the mission of the church to confront social wrongs. Much of the strength of the urban church continues to be supported by that vision. A more recent emphasis has arisen from concern for church growth. When mentioned at all, religious education has most often been seen as a means of helping the church become active in social issues or in winning and keeping members. But religious education is a ministry with its own integrity.

There are all kinds of valid ministries in urban churches. None needs be held up as the one and only form of ministry. It is, in fact, the recognition and endorsement of the incredible variety of urban church ministries that promises hope in the midst of the complexity of world urbanization.

While little attention has been given in print to the peculiar problems and opportunities facing the urban church in its religious education mission, that invisibility should not be the basis for concluding that the people of the church have not been at work, wrestling with issues of education. Faithful teachers have been teaching. Students have been learning amid the perplexing complexities that persist.

Must the church face the educational issues of its urban congregations? The answer is a solid yes. If the church is to be a whole church, if the church is to be effective in the midst of the overwhelming urbanization of the world population, if the church is to build strength into its future, then educational issues must be faced, teachers and administrators and curriculum material writers must be encouraged to continue in their tasks.

The variety that characterizes the urban church carries over into the problem of making sense of the education ministries of the urban churches. Developing some sort of categorizing framework for thinking about urban church education can help us in the process of making decisions about the particular ministry we each must construct for our own particular situation.

One such system of categories which would help us think through the issues of a particular program or larger curriculum plan is based on such critical factors as these developed by D. Campbell Wyckoff:[1]

- What is the purpose of the education ministry? (objective-goals)
- What is to be taught? (scope)
- Who does the teaching? (personnel)
- Where will the education process take place? (context)
- When in the life of the church or the individual does the education take place? (timing)
- What techniques, methods, and relationships are the vehicles of the education? (process)
- What holds it all together? (organizing principle)

James Michael Lee has a similar set of conceptual concepts in his work on the essentials of a model of religion teaching. He writes, "First, the model highlights and accentuates the four major independent variables indispensable to every religious instruction act wherever and whenever this act occurs. These four major variables are the teacher, the learner, the subject matter content, and the environment."[2]

The value of either set of categories is to give the person doing analytical and comparative thought a framework for the reflective process. As Lee demonstrates later in that same volume, the difference between using religious education examples in uncritical duplication and using them as models for thoughtful reinterpretation is crucial. He illustrates this point by showing how we might take one of those two options in an attempt to have Jesus shape our teaching process.[3] The difficulties of exact duplication rest on the intervening variables that must be taken into consideration. Jesus is a useful model when we understand the basic principles of his method and reinterpret those for our day. This is more difficult but more promising than slavish imitation.

A simplistic example of the difference would be to see that Jesus often taught during a walk with his disciples, teaching as the situation required along the way. The slavish imitation would see the modern teacher gathering a small group of about twelve and going off into the city to teach what might come to mind during the walk. As a different and provocative technique, that would have some value. But to say that Jesus taught this way and so all teachers should do the same is to miss the point. By making an abstraction, using the categories above to ask questions about what was going on, we can arrive at the elements of a model: Jesus used the immediate experience and the action of ministry as the basis for religious instruction. We can do the same; walking around in small groups is not the core of the model.

That thought process is advised for those who turn to the chapters in this book that describe programs of religious education. By asking questions, with the guidance of the system of inquiries of Wyckoff or Lee, about both the example given and one's own situation, the connecting principles can be uncovered and the process of model-thinking can lead to insights for new strategies for religious education in whatever situation the reader is situated.

The reader will note that some of the chapters are primarily descriptive of the most common, even belatedly classic forms of religious education. Others have an emphasis that brings to mind the way religious education is part of the outreach ministries of the church. Yet a third emphasis to be found in the following pages places religious education inside of the "public ministry" pattern of church life. In most actual systems of religious education, the programs will be mixtures of these three and other variations and will be distinguishable by major emphases rather than by clear and clean exclusive embodiments.

In the most common forms, that which seems to us to be classic even though its history is relatively short, religious education takes place in a traditional classroom and most often has the intent of handing on the faith. I would say that this is the central form of religious education in our century. It is found in the Sunday school, the parochial school, the CCD program, and the Christian day school.

In this pattern, students are most often grouped by age or "public school" grade level. The subject matter is Bible, tradition, the elements of worship, cognitive doctrine, the principles of behavior in the Christian life, and so forth. In fact, the widespread existence of this way of doing religious education may be one reason it has received so little attention in the recent literature on urban church ministry. Is there a place for this rich, varied, but common form of religious education in our urban churches? The answer must certainly be affirmative. Students, young and old, need to learn and relearn the basic core of our faith. They need to know the Bible, the history, the hymns, the creeds and confessions, the prayers, the worship patterns of the church. This pattern has a proven effectiveness in attaining these goals. Materials are readily available describing the Sunday school, the parochial school, the CCD program, the Christian day school. The task is to make the necessary adaptations for the various urban situations.

When religious education becomes closely identified with outreach ministries we find the process being stretched by both the objectives and the settings. Here we note that the distinguishing characteristic is the conscious implementation of religious education as outreach. The decisions about programming and curriculum materials are shaped by the intent to move out beyond the church family or congregation or parish to those, usually in the neighborhood or "service area," who are not yet fully within the life of the church. In some instances the goal is evangelization or recruitment. In others the goal is equipment for life in ways that are neglected by existing, often secular, educational programs. For years the churches have established life-skills education programs for needy people in places like settlement houses and community centers. Currently churches combine religious education with tutoring assistance. Club programs, general education in religion for the nonaffiliated, and character-building programs with a social or athletic program base are all examples of education as outreach.

When religious education is perceived as part of a "public ministry" emphasis in the church, the program is shaped by the needs of entire congregations reaching for justice in social dimensions. Religious education is characterized by the intent to bring the church into effective ministries of social change. What little attention that has been given to religious education in the literature on urban ministry in the past twenty years has been mostly in this vein. Education for social action, training models for "justice ministries," learning through in-depth involvement in community life are forms of the incorporation of religious education into this pattern of church life and action.

Combinations of these emphases are more often the reality than not. In fact, creative combining of elements from these three and other basic models may well prove to be the most effective means by which we can "particularize" our ministries. The article by Letty Russell tells how in the earlier days of the East Harlem Protestant Parish traditional religious education models were reshaped by community outreach and lay planning to create an effective education ministry.

While imitation may be the sincerest form of flattery, this book is not designed to promote off-the-rack purchase of any particular program. We wish to avoid putting forth some new "fad" for urban church education, some new obligatory program that must be instituted in order to be faithful or successful or, at least, in step with some current-day conceptualization of urban ministry. Rather, if those who read this book are encouraged to examine a program described here, to compare it as a "model of religious education" with their own situation, to combine it with another model as seems fit, to reshape and tailor it through sensitive experimentation, and to share it, imperfections and all, with others, then the education ministry of the urban church will become a cooperative adventure, a pilgrimage toward greater effectiveness.

In addition to the models chapters, other sections of the book are designed to sensitize our awareness of the immediate context in which we educate religiously. These historical and theoretical chapters display, deductively or inductively, an author's exploration and statement of the nature of the religious, social, and cultural dynamics of the urban scene. These authors are not in complete agreement as to what are the most significant factors. That is, these authors reflect their own points of view. Again, their positions, even when stated with some fervor, as the reader will note, are not intended to be normative.

The contributors to this book come from a cross section of the church. They are laity and clergy, men and women, black and white and brown, conservative and liberal, serving in churches and seminaries and national offices across the land from east to west and south to north. What they have in common are experience in the urban church and a commitment to the religious education work of the urban church.

Theory is most useful when it is heuristic, that is, when it stimulates the reader to ask questions and formulate answers that have personal and situational integrity. As I have stated in my theoretical chapter, the development of sets of principles to guide the decision-making process (the development of theory for religious education in the urban church) must ultimately be carried out by those on the front line. I invite you, the reader, to explore this book "in conversation" with your colleagues in urban religious education. They have risked sharing their thoughts and experience because they are committed, as you are, to the presence of Christ's church in the city, and to the nurture of God's people. I also invite you, the reader, to explore this book with your colleagues and friends who are not working in urban settings, so that these persons can become excited about, and maybe even become involved in, urban church education.

Notes

1. D. Campbell Wyckoff, *Theory and Design of Christian Education Curriculum* (Philadelphia: Westminster, 1961); see also James R. Schaeffer, *Program Planning for Adult Christian Education* (New York: Newman, 1972).

2. James Michael Lee, "Religious Education and the Bible: A Religious Educationist's View," in *Biblical Themes in Religious Education,* ed. Joseph S. Marino (Birmingham, Ala.: Religious Education Press, 1983), pp. 40-41.

3. Ibid., pp. 38-47.

Chapter 2

From Setting to Theory: Principles of Urban Church Education

Donald B. Rogers

The development of theory is seen by some religious educators as a process of bringing the insights of various foundational disciplines to bear on the practical processes of religious education. For others, theory is essentially heuristic as it engages religious educators in a dialogue to sharpen the principles that undergird practical decision making. In this chapter my emphasis is upon developing principles out of the practice of religious education. Experience in urban church education is the arena chosen for the exploration of this pattern.

A mere description of a practical entity in religious education, such as a program, can be simply and directly put in place. The problems arise when that direct application of what worked so well in its original setting begins to dysfunction. Then the decison makers face this kind of choice: Move from this experiment to another and then to another, until they stumble on one that works, for a while at least, *or* reflect upon the theory that has explicitly or implicitly guided that copied program and carefully choose, modify, put into operation, evaluate, and gradually improve religious education activity.

In my estimation it is that latter process, guided by a carefully developed theory that is the most practical. But my second thesis is that any truly workable theory must be relevant to the specific situation in which it will be used for guidance. Theory must arise out of the very context in which it will be implemented and must reflect the minds and hopes and experience of the people who will do the implementation.

In this reflection on principles of Christian education for the urban setting I proceed in conformity with the above-mentioned understandings of theory. This is not the usual religious education pattern of theory-to-setting in which a set of foundational ideas becomes the basis for theory which is then applied to the practice of education.[1] Rather, I use an *inductive* approach to theory which seeks to find theory implicit in the practice of religious education, in the setting. In setting-to-theory method, "discovered theory" then becomes the dialogical partner for the more common deductive methods of theorizing. Although I affirm the deductive process of theory development, I believe in the potential value of inductive theory formation as a counterpart and contributor to the whole process.

In addition, I am aware that most written theory has been developed at a level of abstraction and generalization appropriate mostly to those with an ability to use the technical languages and the technical concepts of various disciplines like psychology and sociology and theology. Theory has been the province of academicians, the generalists. Technical theory then has to be more or less successfully translated into ordinary language to make it useful as a guide for church workers. The translated mood is usually prescriptive.

When the development of theory becomes inductive, however, the task of theory development shifts to the parish, to the on-scene practitioners. Academic theoreticians then become assistants to a *descriptive* process. When we realize that those within the setting have the best chance of understanding the intricacies and subtleties of the complex variations that must be taken into consideration in the shaping of theory, then the outside generalist theoretician changes from a generalized prescription maker to a facilitator for understanding that which specifically has been found and described.

When we open up the doors for the indigenization of religious education, for making theory development as well as the implementation of theory the province of the ordinary people who do the educating, then we have a call for the generalist to become the enriching/enriched partner in a two-way conversation. The generalist brings both an ear that is sensitized by the insights of the foundation disciplines and a set of communication skills that are broadly resourceful. It is in that manner that the generalist's contributions can most help in the decisions that must be made by the on-site people in the establishment of goals, methods, and resources. The generalist must be increasingly sensitive to the intricacies of the local situation and increasingly adept in the provision of alternative models of religious education. I see this as the best of both worlds, the frontline practitioner and the professionally trained academician working in a dialogue of respect to address the perplexing issues of urban church education.

A good theory, in any forum, should meet these criteria:

- It should be consistent with supportive and informing general conclusions from the relevant foundation scholarly fields (theology, social science, humanities, etc.).
- It should be sound internally: consistent, comprehensive, parsimonious, and clear.
- It should also provide useful guidance for the practice of education (to the decision-making arena of implementation) and thus be available to the day-by-day practitioners in a largely nontechnical form.

Experiential Factors that Guide Theory

In working from setting-to-theory I must first pay attention to observable factors in various urban church settings where I have either worked or been in conversation with urban church educators.[2] The factors of the actual situations prompt reflection on the process of education and give birth to the principles of theory. These that follow are some of the situational factors that seem important to me.

The factors that have come to my attention include these:

1. Urban church diversity
2. Need for clarity in understanding the setting

3. Wholeness/completeness in our concept of the church
4. Activist captivity of the church
5. Severe limitations in leadership, funding, and facilities
6. Anonymity and distrust influencing surrogate role demands
7. Two-behavior realities
8. The obscuring of the line between general and religious education
9. The irrelevance of resource materials
10. Time-bomb patterns of religious education.

Urban Church Diversity

The place to begin is with the singular complexity and diversity of the urban church and the consequent need to be fully aware of the indigenization of religious education activity. Not only are urban churches characterized by diversity and heterogeneity but the diversity and heterogeneity are simultaneously hidden *and* highly influential in the determination of an education ministry.

Urban churches can look alike, be located in the same neighborhood, share a similar denominational heritage, look back upon overlapping parish histories and yet have very little in common at those levels of reality that will shape the ministry of education. Douglas Walrath's typology as used by C. Kirk Hadaway places thirty-six combination categories before us.[3] When we add such other factors as those related to external demographic patterns, those related to internal demographic and interaction patterns, the perceptual interpretation possibilities of those patterns by the religious education makers, and varieties of understanding of a theological nature, the extent of the diversity becomes apparent.

This diversity shapes the development of theory. It has become the first principle of theory, the first principle of metatheory, if you will, as the theory as well as the practice of religious education has been indigenized. While this metaprinciple is implicitly affirmed in the domain of practice (the indigenization of the practice of religious education being a generally affirmed part of teacher preparation though not identified by name), it has now been extended de facto to include the development of theory.

Factors that follow closely upon those that surround diversity are those that relate to the nature of the church and its mission. For example, I think of a tendency to resist identifying wholeness with completeness, particularly programatic completeness, in the conceptualization of the church.

THE NEED FOR CLARITY
IN UNDERSTANDING THE SETTING

The need to improve our perception of the context in which our ministries take place is a task brought to our attention by those in the field of sociological analysis. The importance of this factor cannot be overstated. Time and again a church fails to see either itself or its immediate context with clear vision. The distortions are often subtle carry-overs from earlier days.

We all know the human tendency to see what we want to see irrespective of what is truly before us. The ironic dimension of this in urban churches is that we as often neglect the promise and the potential of a situation as we neglect the harder realities. We see what we are used to seeing. Our perceptual references come from those times in our past, individually and institutionally, when we experienced the highs and the lows of energy. The "Good Old Days" are legendary in their distortion of both the memory and the comparative tendency.

The church in which I serve as pastor finds energy in remembering some Good Old Days when a group of lay people decided that the children of the neighborhood should have a Sunday school experience even though there was no church at hand. Those lay people organized a school under a tree, and moved to the basement of a home when the weather got bad. Some years later that same Sunday school became the largest in the city. They could bemoan our fall from prominence, or we could rejoice in the courageous vision of the "tree school" and find new ways to see our present situation.

The goal is not just good counting, a fascination with statistics for their own sake. The goal is to have the numbers challenge our vision so that we see reality in all of its provocative dimensions of the good and the bad.

WHOLENESS/COMPLETENESS IN OUR CONCEPT OF THE CHURCH

Some time in this century churches became programing institutions.[4] They became institutions that fulfilled ministries by the development of programs. They became competitors with other churches and nonchurch institutions in program implementation. They developed a position of minister or director of programing. They were evaluated by potential new members on the basis of programatic completeness.

The uncritical identification of wholeness with completeness in this programing modality led some urban churches to despair. Those that had very limited resources (in leadership particularly) could not offer even the minimal range of programs and concluded that they were thus not a whole church.

It became difficult for the people in these situations to make selective decisions among ministries and among parts of any particular ministry without suffering a sense of immediate failure. Finally they began to realize that they need not equate wholeness with completeness. They could think about a whole church that did not have an education ministry to speak of at all. They could see themselves as whole even though not serving a cradle to grave population. They were free to interpret their response to the "need to teach" in a very focused manner. All of this came from a new understanding of the church that did not naively equate completeness with wholeness. This understanding also made it possible to have an appropriate indigenization of theory and practice of education without a strong sense of immediate inadequacy and failure.

It would be a mistake to infer principles of religious education for the urban church without clear identification of the kinds of churches that legitimately are only accidentally urban in setting. We defer to Howard Moody for his distinction between the urban church and the city church.[5] The city church is the church committed to the city and thus, in his vision, able to celebrate the city as sacrament, make symbiosis incarnate, and become the celebrant of change. Not every urban church is or need be a city church.

Urban churches are large as well as small, homogeneous as well as heterogeneous, commuter as well as neighborhood, special interest (Hadaway's term is "exclusive") as well as generalist, rich as well as poor. The large commuter church contributes new patterns in which the education ministry helps to provide human scale experiences. Special interest churches contribute new ways to undergird frontline ministries of deeply committed laity with raised awareness levels and confrontational skills.

Magnificent ministries of music, social witness, symbolic presence, and political effectiveness have within them understanding that enriches the church's religious education perceptions.

THE ACTIVIST CAPTIVITY OF THE CHURCH

Another limiting perception being implicitly challenged by the indigenous theorizing process is most evident in the literature on urban ministry. One of my seminary students, reflecting on her bibliographical research in the literature on urban religious education, called this the "activist captivity of the ideology of the urban church." Those writing about urban ministry, seeing that some urban churches are surrounded by the ills that beset our society, and surrounded by them in such a manner that they cannot overlook them, have become single-minded advocates of social reform ministries for all urban churches. This ideological burden that my student found in the literature on urban ministry at the same time that she found little on religious education as a ministry in the urban church is a burden that needs to be laid aside.

That an activist form of the mission of the church is optional, that it could be chosen rather than imposed, and that it is neither the sole nor the primary sign of faithfulness is a stance that allows the theorizing process to develop an indigenous religious education theory of the church. The people who must live out the life of a church are enabled to come to their own definition of that church and to extrapolate its ministering implications, including those related to religious education.

RESPONDING TO SEVERE LIMITATIONS

Some urban congregations find themselves in the midst of a strength/weakness dilemma. The tendency is to focus on problems in the present while remembering only the strengths of the past. Even present strengths are overshadowed by the memories of days of greater numbers, greater wealth, greater homogeneity, and the like. The present is seen as overwhelmingly rife with problems. It is not uncommon to find urban church educators who suffer from not being able to understand their current situation. The combination of the perceptual impact of memories of strength and the overwhelming nature of the present problems makes it extremely difficult to have a clear stance in respect to a proactive strategy of education. On the one hand we have the opportunity described by Howard Moody:

> The theological meaning of symbiotic (the city is symbiosis) is that it is a metaphor for God's glorious and amazing mix of human creation that we find in the city—the color and shade of skins, the babel of so many languages, the variety of sexes. There can be *no* civilization, no *civitas*, no city without this great human heterogeneity. . . . The loving and caring for that diversity is a human necessity and a divine decree.[6]

On the other hand, the local church which affirms this appreciation of heterogeneity knows just as fully that the past has not prepared its teachers for this new task. All their remembered images of strength and effectiveness are seemingly irrelevant, and all the opportunities of the present are clothed in obscurities. This seems to be particularly true when the heterogeneity of the urban church encloses diversity of lifestyle and diversity of social class.[7]

The principles of religious education that respond to this issue encompass matters of focus, compromise, and development of teacher competency in ways that review the past and provide hope without idealization of the present. To have the courage to focus on the realistic possibilities displayed by a thorough survey of one's present strengths; to do what those allow, and not do all that is known should be done; to use one's past almost brutally in the undergirding of the present, walking away from all nostalgic resting in the past and into the addressing of the present, is the kind of tough relevance that is found in urban churches. This is especially true of those churches that have faced the options of leaving and quitting and have decided to stay and to minister.

As some put it, we do the best we can with what we have in the place we are and let God worry about the rest.

ANONYMITY AND DISTRUST INFLUENCING SURROGATE ROLE DEMANDS

At one time all fourteen of the members of the youth group at one of the churches I served lived in the neighborhood. The reason they came to that church was in large part geographical. Two of those still live in the neighborhood, but only two. The rest have moved away during those high-school years. They are not mobile in the sense that they have easy mobility over the city area. So when they moved (were moved) they lost contact with neighbors and friends and, to some considerable extent, with members of their families. In some instances they lost regular contact with one of their parents. They began a pattern that involves them in mobility, anonymity, and distrust as well as the diversity mentioned above.

They have a great loyalty to their church as a way of keeping some relationships going when others are disrupted. The result is that they have a greater need for stability in those relationships which remain, including those with the leadership and members of the church. This need is sometimes expressed in the form of an almost surrogate parent expectation which they bring to adults in the church. The surrogate relationship is demanding. It takes time and emotional energy. Most adults cannot handle more than a few of these relationships, and the leader/student ratio must be kept low.

A worker in a neighborhood club model of urban ministry commented that the permanency of relationships they seek to provide there may be *the* major factor in their work. "These kids are always leaving, it seems, or being left. We stay around."[8]

Some urban situations require anonymity for survival. One cannot handle close relationships with the numbers of people who are present in a daily pattern of urban interaction. Yet, the very anonymity patterns that make survival possible undercut the possibilities of significant, lasting, intimate friendships. This factor, combined with that of mobility, further enforces the need for a steady presence and low student/teacher ratio.

The lower ratio makes it possible for students to overcome the hesitancies in the relationship areas and for the leaders to have the emotional stamina sufficient to respond to the relationship expectations once those hesitancies are overcome.

Mobility and anonymity have another effect. They are accompanied by distrust. The particular dimension of distrust being identified here is a general one seen as a disproportionate reaction to real causes for fear and anxiety. The same distorted portrayals of urban life that keep some people from living, working, or even visiting the urban setting are read and heard and seen by urbanites. When the church is not able, along with other agencies and institutions, to broadcast "alternate news" (Howard Moody's phrase) along with God's Good News and establish cohesion patterns that will allay fears to an appropriate proportionality, then the education ministry faces a credibility problem. Credibility is made up of factors of time, stability, realism, and presence as well as factors of knowledge and skill in subject matter areas.

TEACHING IN A TWO-BEHAVIOR WORLD

Urban church educators worry about education for victimization. There are times when they fear that they are insensitive to the reality of a "two-behavior" world in which their students must live. Behavior education, socialization in the role expectations appropriate to Christian discipleship, can be uncritically generalized by some students, particularly the young ones, in a manner that increases the likelihood that they will become victims. Thus some urban religious educators consciously adopt and teach in a sanctuary model that allows a two-behavior system to exist without increasing internal contradictions.

OBSCURING THE LINE BETWEEN GENERAL
AND RELIGIOUS EDUCATION

Another issue that arises is the need to obscure the dividing lines between what might be thought to be the legitimate domain of public education and that thought to be the predominant domain of church education. In some urban situations the most redeeming teaching may well have to include the subject matters of life's basic skills. To teach to read, to do basic arithmetic, to plan for a career, to take on adult responsibilities as a child or youth, to learn the skills needed to confront slow and insensitive systems—all of these seem not to be in the curriculum resources issued by the denominational publishing houses or by independent publishers of religious education curricula.

The fact is a lot of people do not read very well, and a good percentage of them are in urban settings and urban churches. Some youths still graduate from high school barely functionally literate. Some older adults never had the opportunity as children to learn to read.

Teaching procedures being developed in response to this situation are radically oral in nature. It is one thing for literate people to increase their appreciation of the "oral tradition." It is quite something else to engage in teaching/learning as well as corporate worship on a completely print-free basis. The key is the oral repetition of a repertoire of basic resources (scriptures, hymns, prayers). The repertoire principle calls for the continuous relearning of all the materials so that they are not lost.

THE IRRELEVANCE OF RESOURCE MATERIALS

A common comment by urban church school teachers on religion curriculum resources is, "Our students can't find themselves in these materials." The diversity and heterogeneity of some urban churches exacerbates the resources problem. The challenges that face the writers and publishers of religion curriculum resources are legion. It seems unrealistic to expect that any set of materials will be able to satisfy the needs of this arena of religious education activity. Even the good faith efforts of some religious publishers to be as sensitive as possible and provide supplementary materials has not solved the problems. The result is that most of the effective curricula and instructional resources are prepared at the local church level.

Some issues are extremely difficult to address in published materials without appearing to be insensitive. The response by on-site urban religious educators seems to have become that the trusted teacher who has established credibility with the learners can create a plan and develop supportive materials as needed in a manner that cannot be generalized. Particular practices cannot be generalized. Only theory possesses the power of generalizability. Thus any highly particularized curricular or instructional practice developed in a specific urban church setting, even though it is very successful, will typically not work or will not work well in a different church situation. Small wonder, then, that there is a reluctance of on-site urban religious educators to share their curricular and instructional resources which they themselves shared with another similar church situation. There is, however, an observed reluctance on the part of the on-site resource producers to share their final products with anyone outside their settings. This reluctance is not just about materials developed to enhance the teaching around sensitive issues.

What these on-site curriculum resource preparers do, by necessity and often with skill, has not become an activity in which they have the confidence that allows them to share. The issues are confidence and permission—*perceived* permission. Without a conscious awareness of a theory of curriculum development and without any deliberative preparation in how to develop curricula, laity are developing curriculum resources in response to need. What *they* need is a statement on the method of curriculum resourcing that endorses the local site production of materials and further trains "ordinary teachers" to engage in the writing and editing tasks.[9]

Some of these locally written curriculum resources are placing a renewed emphasis on a basic, wisdom-like, set of materials. A core of documents is being culled out as an essential curriculm that parallels or works within all other plans over all the childhood to young adult years. Such a curriculum is also being used to bring new adult believers into a basic literacy of the church's literature. What the extent of this movement is is not known. Its existence is significant.

TIME-BOMB PATTERNS IN URBAN RELIGIOUS EDUCATION

Time-Bomb Patterns in Urban Religious Education

Time-bomb religious education came to my attention from those people who reflected back over a lifetime in which, with the church's help, they had climbed out of an urban situation of profound poverty to more than nominal success in various careers. Their reflections were prompted by the price they found they had paid for that success, a price in physical maladies that began to appear in the later stages of their lives.

For these people, the church, primarily in its religious education work, had been the strong base for the acquisition of a sense of personal identity and pride, together with the hope for a life beyond that in which they had lived as children. They found the vision and the strength to break a cycle of poverty through the church. What they did not know along the way until too late was that their whole-hearted commitment to career and family and church, unrelieved by any sense of the sabbatical life, led them, quite willingly they would point out, to a lifestyle that was a time-bomb of destruction. They had worked so hard on all of the days of the week for so many years that they had no sense of the sabbath-like quiet and calm that could bring healing into their lives. They learned a lifestyle that became destructive, the more so because it was a set of habits implicitly endorsed by the church.

The church needs to understand the complexities of the patterns of life which it endorses and become aware of delayed consequences. The encouragements which students remember from their pasts may need to be repeated. It may be possible, however, to reduce the destructive elements along the way. Stackpole's emphasis on the absolute necessity for a carefully thought through and implemented process of reentry for those involved in intense camping experiences is another dimension of this issue.

IN SUMMARY

While it seems necessary to conclude this chapter with a summation of the principles discussed in the light of various factors in urban religious education practice, the effort is not intended to suggest that we have displayed a theory. If this work has merit, more careful listening to religious educators in urban church settings is required. The accumulation of more principles and the integration of them into a whole piece would be the beginning of the set, the theory.

In review, I see the following as main principles of religious education in the urban church:

1. Theory can and indeed does arise out of the local existential setting and has the advantage of being particularly relevant to the diversity present in the urban setting.
2. Principles can be framed within a broad range of understandings of the nature and mission of the church and be valid in even highly limited and focused interpretations.
3. Not every church in the city is a city church and religious education activity can and does reflect the unique character of non-city urban churches.
4. The decision makers for urban religious education must have a sense of freedom from stereotypes of church and religious education so that they can be exceedingly realistic in the decisions they must make in the face of severe limitations.
5. Teacher/student ratios may need to be reduced significantly in order to provide intense surrogate relationships needed by the students.
6. Some settings have multiple role and behavior expectations, so that Christian lifestyle nurturing is sometimes intentionally dual.
7. What is to be taught is being defined holistically. Sometimes this places an emphasis upon subjects and skills that are not specifically thought of as within the scope of "regular" religious education. Radically oral materials and methods are needed in some settings.
8. Many resources are better produced within the setting of

their intended usage by the teachers who can respond with sensitivity and credibility to the issues of the time and place.
9. Some lifestyle patterns are unavoidable compromises between destructive options. Awareness of this dilemma may in itself be a partial solution.

The development of theory in the urban settings is a faithful response to the call to the church to teach. Those who wrestle with the issues, the dynamics, the challenges, and the blessings speak to the church at large.

Notes

1. See Donald B. Rogers, *Analogous Reasoning and the Problem of Correlation in Christian Education Theory* (Ph.D. dissertation, Princeton Theological Seminary, 1967). I have used the inductive pattern in two books: *In Praise of Learning* (Nashville: Abingdon, 1980) and *Teachable Moments* (Nashville: Discipleship Resources, UMC, 1986).
For a brief summary of the nature of theory and how it has the power of generalizability, see James Michael Lee, "The Authentic Source of Religious Instruction," in *Religious Education and Theology*, ed. Norma H. Thompson (Birmingham, Ala.: Religious Education Press, 1982), pp. 117-121.
2. My experience includes professional staff involvement in urban churches in Colorado Springs, Colorado; East Orange, New Jersey; Dayton, Ohio; and Cincinnati, Ohio. I have been in conversation with people in urban settings in Mississippi, Georgia, Michigan, Indiana, Iowa, Kentucky, and Tennessee. The churches are affiliated with the AME, AME Zion, American Baptist, Church of God, Disciples, Episcopal, Independent Baptist, Lutheran, Presbyterian, Roman Catholic, Southern Baptist, UCC, and UMC traditions.
3. Douglas A. Walrath, "Social Change and Local Churches: 1951-1975," in *Understanding Church Growth and Decline*, ed. Dean R. Hoge and David A. Rogen (New York: Pilgrim, 1979), pp. 248-269. See also C. Kirk Hadaway, "Church Growth (and Decline) in a Southern City," *Review of Religious Research* 23 (June, 1982), pp. 372 ff. See also Warren J. Hartman, "Five Audiences," *Discipleship Trends* I (1983).
4. See Howard L. Grimes, "Church Education: A Historical Survey and a Look to the Future," *Perkins School of Theology Journal* (Spring, 1972), p. 30.
5. Howard Moody, "In Praise of the City," *Metropolitan Ministries*

Team, ed. Yamina Apolinaris (American Baptist Church National Ministries),third page (unnumbered pages).

6. Ibid., second page.

7. See Arnold Mitchell, *The Nine American Lifestyles: Who We Are and Where We Are Going* (New York: Macmillan, 1983). This is a value-based analysis yielding four major categories and nine lifestyles. They are titled, *Need Driven: Survivor, Sustainer; Outer-Directed: Belonger, Emulator, Achiever; Inner-Directed: I-Am-Me, Experiential, Societally Conscious; Combined Outer-Inner: Integrated.* This is a particularly helpful method for seeing the internal dynamics of the church over against the external situation.

8. Interview with Steve Jacobs, CURE (Christians United Reaching Everyone) a neighborhood club and summer camp ministry located in the Over-the-Rhine and Pendleton neighborhoods of Cincinnati, Ohio. Comment made in an urban education seminar in Cincinnati in 1985 sponsored by the Council of Christian Communions and United Theological Seminary.

9. See Donald B. Rogers, *The Way of the Teacher* (Nashville: Discipleship Resources, UMC, 1985) on the value of the ordinary in the teacher.

Chapter 3

Christian Religious Education and the Inner City

Letty M. Russell

Twenty-two years have passed since I wrote this article in a book entitled *An Introduction to Christian Education*. A great deal of change has come about in our cities, nation, and world. Yet the basic problems and opportunities of the inner city remain. The problems are even worse today. In spite of strong efforts at urban renewal and planning in the 1960s and early 1970s, we find ourselves with more homeless people than ever before. Buildings are closed by the city, and funds are not used to rehabilitate them, while other more attractive urban housing is turned over to condominiums and gentrification. The net result is that many urban areas in the United States resemble urban ghettos of the so-called "underdeveloped nations."

In the face of these devastating circumstances of homelessness, poverty, hunger, overcrowding, drugs, and wasted lives, a discussion of church school curriculum seems to be of little consequence. Yet the people who dwell in East Harlem, New York, and other urban slums still long to hear the Good News that they are "somebody" in God's sight. This search for meaning and hope in one's life is a genuine call to the church for concrete social witness and action, day by day. As communities of faith and hope within each one of these struggling ghetto communities, church families are still called to listen and learn

from people in the inner city in "working out patterns of Christian education which are suited to the culture of the inner city"
[269].

Writing this article today, I would most certainly place even
more emphasis on social and economic analysis of the "Problems and Opportunities in the Inner City." Another change
[made in this edition: ed.] is to use inclusive language rather
than male generic language in referring to God and persons.
Thus I describe religious education as joining in "God's work of
restoring [people] to their true, created humanity by reconciling them to [Godself] and to one another" [269]. Third, I would
not consider myself qualified to write such an article today
because, after seventeen years of working in East Harlem, I
began teaching in college and seminary in 1960. While I can
still be an advocate for justice and liberation among the peoples of the inner city, I am no longer an active participant,
listener, and learner in their daily lives.

In spite of a shift in context, my basic understanding of religious education and the life of the Christian community has not
changed. I still believe in the importance of peer teaching and
learning and continue to employ this educational philosophy in
my seminary classroom as I teach and practice liberation and
feminist theology.

Religious Education and the Inner City

The shape of religious education today emerges out of the
process of dialogue between our faith in Jesus Christ as Lord
and our understanding of the world in which we live.

The term "inner city" in this chapter will be used to describe
the forgotten world of poverty which lies at the center of all our
large cities. Such areas of poverty are the dwellings built as
immigrant housing or left behind in the middle-class retreat
from the city but now inhabited by minority groups who have
neither the power nor the money to break out of the city
ghettos. Here all the problems of city life are mirrored at their
worst. Here the church as an institution has as much trouble
finding "answers" as any other city institution, be it the welfare
department, housing authority, or board of education.

In the inner city there are certain social problems which

affect the work of the church in religious education. First, there are large numbers of children ready and eager to come to the programs. For instance, in the seven-block area surrounding the Church of the Ascension which I serve live over 16,000 people. Large numbers of children find themselves with nothing to do and will come to the church to be "entertained" if given half a chance. Second, there is always a discipline problem. The families themselves are full of stresses and strains which produce behavior problems. The child seldom receives training in self-discipline either at home or at school. Third, according to middle-class social standards, the life of the children and their families is amoral. In communities where the struggle for existence is so real that everyone learns to lie and cheat and steal as a matter of course, the standard of behavior is "What's in it for me?" The kind of "be good" teaching which is found in most Sunday schools is at best ineffective, and more often hypocritical in such a situation. Fourth, the children lack family encouragement. It is simply ridiculous to expect the family to be the mainstay of religious education.[1] The family has a hard time staying together at all. Children are fed and clothed and then left to entertain themselves. Lastly, there is predominantly a lack of education among parents and children alike. Parents have not had educational advantages which would enable them to teach their children a love of learning and of ideas. The types of questions which religious educators often imagine a child might want to discuss in class would never even occur to the parent, let alone the child. And the children also are forced to accept inferior education as they attend ghetto schools which are warped by the woeful inadequacies of outworn, bureaucratic, or irrelevant systems of education.

The inner-city church brings certain practical problems of its own to the task which it faces. Not only does it feel defeated by the community problems but also by its own lack of resources to work in and through these problems. Church staffs are usually limited because of lack of funds and lack of vocational opportunities for advancement. Religious teachers are few in number. Most people with natural ability are usually very busy working overtime or on two jobs, and others, who are forced to

struggle for existence on welfare because of their many problems, find themselves unable or unwilling to cope with other
people's children and with curriculum outlines they often cannot even read. The church buildings are usually old and inadequate, having either too much or too little space. Physical
plants, already run-down with neglect and disuse, begin to
deteriorate rapidly when their doors are opened to large
groups of children and youth.

The religious educator who truly desires to make religious
education a living and vital part of a Christian community will
do well to follow these four steps: 1) Don't sit down and weep,
for a vast world of wonderful people and unknown resources is
open to all who would follow Christ out into the world where
he lived and died. 2) Live in and with your community. Study
and learn about your community and its culture. Listen with an
open mind, and love the city and its people with an open heart.
You will often find that what you thought was apathy was
simply the community's refusal to respond to the middle-class
blueprint of church life which you brought with you. Together
with the members of the community seek out the real problems which you face. 3) Continue to let your understanding of
the Christian faith grow and mature as you struggle with what
the gospel message means for this time and place. 4) Turn the
problems of the community to advantage by working out patterns of religious education which are suited to the culture of
the inner city where you live and serve.

Religious Education in the Context of Total Church Life

The shapes of religious education should take form in a situation of dialogue between theology and sociology.

Religious education is the work of the church in extending
Christ's invitation to all men, women, and children to join in
God's work of restoring people to their true, created humanity
by reconciling them to Godself and to one another. This means
that the church invites men, women, and children not only to
let the love of Christ work in them to shape their lives by his
love, but also to join in Christ's action to bring about reconciliation and wholeness to all of society. In order to extend this
invitation, the church must make itself continually aware of the

way God has revealed Godself in the past by thorough study of the biblical record. At the same time it must make itself continually aware of the way God is acting in the events of our own time through careful study of the issues which confront people today. With the eyes of faith to search our God's actions of judgment and reconciliation in the world, the church may be able to point to this activity of God by the integrity of its own life as a Christian family and by its involvement in the work of Christ's healing and reconciliation in its own community.

Thus religious education involves three dimensions: the work of opening people's eyes to see God's activity, helping them find ways to join in this activity in the world, and pointing to this activity so that others may see and receive the invitation to be partners with God. Nurture or the "equipping of the saints" takes place continually in the light of the invitation to join in God's action both as preparation for and through involvement in that action. Martin Luther has said that no one is ever a Christian—each is only on the way to becoming a Christian. This is why the invitation to join in God's work must be extended over and over, in, with, and during every task which a Christian congregation undertakes. Then it may be continually strengthened in its insight, its faith, and its service to the world in the name of Jesus Christ. The work of extending this invitation is the job of the total church congregation—the job of religious education.

In the light of this definition of religious education it becomes clear that a program of religious education can never be separated from the rest of the life and witness of a congregation except for the purpose of planning and evaluation. A church family is needed to strengthen the weak families where they exist and to be the Christian family to those who have no other. In such a family the invitation may be heard by those who have been told by society that they are worthless. Here they learn that their service is needed, that they indeed can be part of the high calling of Christ's mission. In such a family the invitation may be heard by people who have learned the hard way that you have to look out for yourself and your own because no one else cares. Here they find other men and women who really do care—care enough to visit in their homes; care enough to work with their children; care enough to fight for better schools, housing, and government; care enough so that they can begin to dare to believe that God cares. In such a family the invitation may be heard by people who are so chained by their problems that the best they can do is sit and wait for each problem to come. Here they find a church family full of the same problems of broken homes, narcotics addiction, delinquency, emotional disturbance, finances, and health. But they find that these people are helping one another bear these burdens. Together they are helping with family and financial problems, helping young people in trouble find mental and medical help. And the people who have been chained find their chains growing lighter as they begin to lift the load of others in the services of Jesus Christ. In such a family the invitation may be heard by men and women who have been taught destructive and self-defeating habits of life by their culture of poverty. Here they find people living in the same culture who have been able to develop at least the beginning of new habits of Christian living which help them resist the pressures all around them. Extending Christ's invitation to join in God's action of reconciliation is the work of the entire church family because this is where the invitation is heard and lived so that others might also hear and live it.

If the total church is to be the instrument of religious education, certain principles follow in terms of specific programing. The first is that the church family should involve children and youth as much as possible in its ongoing life of worship and service to the world. Children should be welcomed and encouraged to attend worship, and the worship should contain enough dramatic content and congregational participation so that it is of interest to the children. The same is true for service in the world. Great effort should be made to let the children help make signs for a picket line, or put out flyers for a rally, and so on. Youth should be encouraged to overcome their own feelings of defeat, failure, and antagonism toward the world by working actively for civil rights and other community causes. Thus the children and youth, as well as adults, learn by doing and sharing together in Christ's mission.

The second principle is that the study of the mighty acts of

God as revealed in the Bible should be planned in such a way that all the different ages and groups in the church are studying the same theme. As people struggle with the same text and its meaning for their life, many new insights are gained. In the East Harlem Protestant Parish the churches follow a *Daily Bible Reading* lectionary which is designed for Bible-study groups and preaching in inner-city churches.[2] Here the same text is studied by staff and Bible-study leaders on Monday, by all the house Bible-study groups on Wednesday, by the children and youth on Sunday, and is the basis for the sermon. Amazing variety is found in interpretations and uses, yet, often just because the word had been listened to so often with such seriousness, God grants new gifts of understanding of purpose for this world.

When the total church is the instrument of Christian education, a third principle emerges. The pastor or associate pastor of the church must be centrally involved in the planning and execution of the religious education program and in working out a consistent theology and plan of religious education in the church family. A church family capable of hearing the invitation of Christ to join in God's action of reconciliation in the world, and/or sharing that invitation with others, grows slowly and develops a pattern of Christian involvement and service in the world through patient years of tender loving care. The pastor or associate pastor who views preaching and an adult Bible-study class as his or her share in religious education has missed the whole point. As long as there is a pastor, the total life of the church cannot be an instrument of education unless the minister sees this and seeks to put it into practice by a direct participation, as well as by cooperating with others who may be hired especially to work in the religious education program.

When the total church is the instrument of religious education, a fourth principle emerges. Religious education is the work of the total church and should involve the total budget. No longer does the religious education item mean a small sum for paper and crayons. The question of how a church raises and distributes its money should be examined in the light of the question of whether it is enabling the church to extend Christ's invitation to join in God's work of reconciliation. Beyond this, the budget should recognize that the work of specific programs of education such as Christian action workshops, Bible-study groups, remedial reading clinics, church school, and youth programs all deserve an important share of the church funds.

THE PEER GROUP AS TEACHER IN WORK WITH CHILDREN AND YOUTH

Those who live in the inner city are by and large "mass people" whose lives are conditioned by peer groups and by group pressures of society. We have already noted the opportunity which this situation provides in working with adults and children in the context of the total church family life. The importance of the church community in the support it gives to individuals was underscored. Here I would like to emphasize the importance of the peer group in work with children and youth. Children and youth dress, talk, and act like their friends. Wearing heavy rubber rain coats in hot summer weather or sneakers in a blizzard is normal behavior if that happens to be the style. Going places together is the only way children and youth are willing to go. The more crowded a candy store, teenage hangout, or church canteen, the more they want to go because "everyone is there."[3]

Any specialized religious education programing for children and youth should take the peer group and peer-group behavior into account unless it wishes to be ineffective before it even begins. For the peer group, rather than being a negative factor in religious education, has great possibilities in helping the church face the problems described above. The problem of amorality can be faced only on a large group basis, for the only way it is possible to change the habits and style of inner-city people is to help a group of people change together so that they do not feel that they are alone in what they are doing. If it were the style to study hard and work to get ahead in school, many wonderful things could happen to our children's school records. If it were the style to save money rather than to spend it on show items and food, the financial patterns of at least one group of inner-city children and youth could be altered. If self-love carried with it the desire to share this love with others, the selfish patterns of living could be revolutionized. This, of course, calls for large groups of children and a strong community of leadership which is able to set and maintain a particular style.

The problem of large numbers of children and youth thus already appears to have some advantage if it were not for the difficulty of dealing with a large group in terms of limitations of space, disciplinary control, and teaching staff. But a large group of from fifty to one hundred children and youth can be handled in one or two moderately large rooms. They like to be together. In fact, they like to be crowded. Given some skill in leadership and group dynamics, the problems of discipline tend to decrease rather than increase when a large group of children is together. A pattern can be set for the group by a consistent routine and schedule and the following of certain basic rules of safety and behavior which will be enforced by the majority of the group itself.

One of the most important characteristics of the peer group is that it teaches itself. Children learn from peers the very information which fell on deaf ears when spoken by adults. In teaching a large group the one teacher can help the children share together in their learning in such a way that through dramas, quiz shows, craft projects, questions and answers, they teach one another.

The basic curriculum of a group program has three elements: the church family, fun, and the Bible. Unless this program is part of the life of a church family which is constantly seeking to serve Christ and invite others to hear and constantly seeking to involve the children in its work and witness and family life, it will fail. For children sense hypocrisy very easily. They live with it every day. And the invitation of Christ which is extended to them is no invitation at all unless it is issued from a church community which has integrity in its life and work. Children and youth need their own programs and own peer groups, but these need to be part of a larger church family which cares about them.

Fun is also a crucial element in the curriculum, for learning is at its maximum when children are enjoying it and participating in it. This can be seen in our own childhood experiences.

Learning by doing is not only helpful to children who cannot read well but also is essential if it is to be fun for children. An important aspect of this is craft projects which teach the lesson but at the same time are fun to make and valued possessions. These projects cost more and take more time to prepare but often can be made of discarded materials. Another equally important source of fun and participation is skits on Bible stories or life situations which can be practiced briefly. The children do not have rigidly memorized lines, but "ad lib" and generally enjoy showing off to their peers. Two other sources of joy are singing songs[4] with good rhythm and quiz shows.

Christ's invitation to join in God's action of reconciliation comes to all of us from the Bible, and it is from the Bible that the history of salvation must be learned. As children grow to adulthood, they will be helped to respond to Christ's invitation if the history of salvation is already part of their life and learned and lived out in the church community of which they are a part. In using a biblically centered curriculum, the life situation of the children and youth is not ignored. Now life is viewed from the perspective of God's action in the past and present.

One example of church family, fun, and Bible will help show how these things go together to make a curriculum. In the East Harlem Protestant Parish for thirteen weeks the whole church studied Exodus and the story of freedom.[5] When it came time for the sixteenth anniversary of the parish we decided to celebrate with a worship service and a family potluck dinner for two hundred people. The theme of the dinner became "Sixteen Years in the Wilderness." Decorations, music, etc., were arranged accordingly. The youth who had also studied Exodus collected all the skits they had done into one long drama of freedom, complete with Moses in a baby carriage, a bush equipped with a burning blowtorch, a cardboard sea, and Miriam's dancers. Everyone enjoyed the play immensely, even when the bush nearly burned up, and the youth had a chance to make a real contribution to their church family. The children were thoroughly involved, for they had also studied Exodus, and most of the scenery had been made by them. The next day two four-year-olds who had attended the festivities were overheard talking together. One child dressed in a green bathrobe said to the one in a red bathrobe, "Will you let my people go?" The red-robed boy replied, "Yes," to which the child in green said with great disgust, "You're not supposed to say that!"

TEAM TEACHING AND TRAINING
IN THE PEER GROUP APPROACH

One possible answer to the shortage of teachers is to recognize that the church has aggravated this problem out of all proportion by thinking that all teaching and all teachers have to fit a certain middle-class pattern. We have assumed that each teacher must learn to be punctual and regular; skilled at discipline; and trained to read, digest, and teach a written curriculum. The result is a great cry that curricula for the white middle-class suburbs are no good in the inner city. Instead of making the teachers over into poor copies of middle-class, college educated teachers, why not uncover and utilize the strengths they do in fact possess? The staff of one such program at the Church of the Ascension consisted of myself as leader, another minister as disciplinarian, the church custodian, the church secretary, parents, and youth assistants.[6]

The peer-group method of teaching with large groups of children affords many opportunities to play to the strengths of the inner-city teacher. It permits the teacher to work with the children so that the teacher can make use of his or her knowledge and experience of the children's culture in relating to them without having to assume a pseudo-role. In the program, emphasis is always put on ways children with leadership ability can form the teaching core both informally through group participation, skits, and so on, and formally when they are selected to work as assistant teachers in a particular program. The best teachers for youth are youth or young adults who are slightly older. These are the ones who set the patterns every day on the streets and who can communicate best with those whom they teach. This also gives the younger teachers valuable experience in their responsibility to serve others as a part of the church family. Lastly, peer-group teaching makes it possible for a teacher to be a valuable part of a Christian education program even if he cannot read a lesson plan.

In peer-group teaching "in-service training" for the teachers is the best method. First, this form of teaching takes place in the context of the total church life as the teacher. Those who come forward to teach are already being nurtured and sustained in other parts of the church family life. The lessons which are taught to children and youth are the same themes that the teacher meets through his or her entire church life. The teacher has the opportunity to explore their meaning in house Bible-study groups and to share insights gained in the teaching program with his or her house group. The teacher knows that questions raised concerning the meaning of a particular text will often receive attention in the sermon. The interaction of thought and experience around one theme gives to the teacher a foundation of training which continues week after week.

Second, a teacher can begin to serve right away with no training or skill at all. As a part of a team, one can find the job best suited to one's ability and knowledge, be it taking attendance, making Kool-ade, preparing crafts, or simply sitting with the children and joining them in singing, discussing, and working together. The teacher is free to learn new skills and greater self-confidence and enters into new areas of teaching, such as planning, leading worship, coaching and acting, running visual-aid equipment, and so on. The teacher learns more quickly if given help and encouragement because he or she has others who are doing it also and does not have to sink or swim alone.

Third, because the emphasis is largely on helping the peer group teach itself, any older person who cares about the children and enjoys being and working with them will bring to the peer-group program what it needs most—encouragement of the children to participate in and enjoy the program and a "leaven" of adult responsibility in the larger group which will free the children from the need to misbehave. In a peer-group program ten adult or youth teachers working and participating and sitting with the children will be sufficient to maintain the order needed with only occasional assistance from the trouble shooter and the person directing the program.

It is possible to run a peer-group program with little or no group planning. One person can plan the entire program, and the teachers can be prepared the half hour before the program begins. Although adult leaders in the inner city are very shy about performing in front of a group or leading a group, some will come to join with the children, youth, and young adults who love to show off and perform in front of the group in skits and panels, and so on. Others who never worked with children before will learn to help a small group put on a program for the larger group. Children love to see their teachers making fools of themselves in a play or funny program. The teachers themselves can plan "take-offs" on the children or simply enter into a game such as Truth or Consequences with the children in which they have to sit on a child's lap or hop around the room once.

Team planning and teaching does not need to ignore the value of small groups and individual attention. It merely puts them in a larger framework. In fact, the group approach is not fully adequate unless the teachers do give children individual attention. A child needs to know that someone in particular cares about him or her, by name, notices the absence and wants to help with the work. Children naturally relate to a particular teacher and tend to seek that teacher out even if they are not assigned to that teacher's table. To aid in this individual concern it is advisable to assign the teachers to particular age groups. Then they are able to develop personal contacts by working more closely with certain children, taking them on trips, entertaining them in their homes, planning skits together, helping them with crafts, and visiting their families. Such personal interest increases the enjoyment and the feeling of worth and importance of both the child and the teacher. Team teaching and planning will help children and teachers alike develop a spirit of cooperation as they work together to make their own program a success. They become a family within a church family which has a particular job to do and enjoys doing it together.

Notes

This article, revised for publication in the present volume, was originally published in *An Introduction to Christian Education*, ed. Marvin Taylor (Nashville: Abinndod, 1966), pp. 267-277.

1. Cf. Letty M. Russell, "The Family and Christian Education in Modern, Urban Society," *Union Seminary Quarterly Review* 16 (November, 1960), pp. 33-43.

2. Letty M. Russell, *Daily Bible Readings, Inner City Parishes*, East Harlem Protestant Parish, 2050 Second Avenue, New York, issued quarterly.

3. *Youth in the Ghetto* (New York: Harlem Youth Opportunities Unlimited, 1964), pp. 370-371.

4. *Alleluia, A Hymnbook for Inner City Parishes*, East Harlem Protestant Parish, 2050 Second Ave., New York, N.Y.

5. Russell, *Daily Bible Readings*.

6. Letty M. Russell, "Equipping the Little Saints, An Emerging Pattern of Christian Education," *Adult Teacher*, (Nashville: Board of Education of The Methodist Church, January-February, 1962).

Chapter 4

Glimpses of the Kingdom in the Urban Church

Chris Michael

In a very large, cosmopolitan city, a cat was rapidly chasing a mouse down a busy street. The cat was bigger, stronger, and faster. The gap between them all but closed. Suddenly the mouse saw a manhole cover with a tiny opening, just large enough for the mouse to slip down to safety. As he crouched inside, shaking in fear, he looked up to see the eye of the hungry cat peering down at him. The mouse waited in the hole for awhile, catching its breath. Before long, it heard the sound of a dog barking. Relieved that the dog had now chased the cat away, the mouse ambled into the sunlight, only to be grabbed up by the ingenious cat who said to the mouse, "In order to survive in this city, you gotta be bilingual."

For much of our denomination's history, we have been monolingual. We have spoken only the language of rural life. Carl Bowman's research on the Church of the Brethren tells us that only 15 percent of us live in the city; the rest of us live in small towns or rural areas. That is nearly the opposite of the total U.S. population which has 75 percent of its citizens living in cities and 25 percent in rural areas. The decline in the membership of the Church of the Brethren has paralleled the decline of rural population in the United States.

While a considerable amount of American church history—

41

especially Protestantism—has been rural, a great deal of the history of Christianity has been in cities. If we look at the Book of Acts, how did the early church grow? Clearly, the growth of the early church followed the contours of the urbanized Roman Empire. The earliest apostles and disciples intentionally moved into the hearts of cities to tell the Good News. They went to the markets, synagogues, and busy streets of cities like Corinth, Philippi, Ephesus, and Rome. The gospel was born in the city of Jerusalem and exploded in growth throughout a chain of cities across the Roman Empire. Consequently, we cannot name a church in the New Testament that was not in a city. Until the fourth century, Christianity was almost exclusively urban.

In order to survive in the next century, we need to learn to be bilingual. We need to learn to speak the language of the city as well as the language of rural areas.

Important questions to ask ourselves are: Where is it that God is calling us? What does obedience to God say to us as we ponder our future? What is our place in urban church ministry?

A Scriptural Mandate

Hebrews 11 is an important scripture for the Church of the Brethren as we think about our future. Our situation is similar to Abraham's. We, too, stand at a decision-making time. Will we stay where it is familiar and comfortable? Or will we go forth in faith to cities filled with people . . . people for whom Christ also came, and lived, and died?

In chapter 11, the writer of Hebrews looks back at the story of Abraham and other forebears of the faith. The writer describes the faith of persons who had gone before such as Abel, Noah, and Enoch, and who had persevered by faith in God's promises. In telling the story of Abraham sojourning to the Promised Land in obedience to God's call, the writer uses the image of the city to describe the Promised Land. Scriptures refer to the city over 1400 times. Scriptures also speak of the city as a place of evil and sin. Also a part of the biblical story, however, are scriptures like Revelation 21 in which John depicts the kingdom coming down from heaven in the form of a city—the New Jerusalem—a place in which there will be no more tears, no more pain, where God will wipe away every tear from our eyes. The kingdom of God is the city of hope.

Taking Risks

The writer says Abraham could have returned home, but he pressed forward toward the promise of a city which has foundations, whose builder and maker is God—a city of hope! Abraham's story can teach us how to minister and teach in the cities of today. As I think about the meaning of the story, I find three learnings which are helpful to our denomination as we seek to be faithful in our times.

The first is that Abraham took an enormous risk. He left behind his homeland, its comfort and familiarity. His obedience to God meant that he risked his present security for an unknown future. As a church, we too are called to risk in obedience to God.

A lively debate stormed on the pages of our news document, the old *Gospel Messenger*, during the turn of this century. Like some of the controversies that spice today's Letters to the Editor, there were emotional exchanges over the urban missions started by our denomination. Some writers insisted that the city is also within the realm of God's love and care and, therefore, ought to be within ours as well. Others wrote that it was too evil, beyond redemption, and a place of temptations. Besides, some said, we know how to be the church in rural areas; we ought to just stick to what we know.

It is easier and more comfortable to stay just as we have always been. The Hebrews 11 passage, however, challenges us to risk, like Abraham, in order to be obedient to God and to open ourselves up to glimpses of God's kingdom. If it is true that God loves all people, and cares for all of the world, then it is time for us to risk being in ministry in places and ways that are not always familiar to us.

Recall Søren Kierkegaard's parable about a flock of geese that lived together in a close, harmonious fellowship in the safety of a fine barnyard. Once a week one of their number would climb up on the barnyard fence and tell the other geese about the joys and wonders of flight and how they, like all geese, were made for something more than a barnyard existence. As he preached, his hearers would often nod in approval and flap their wings as a sign of their agreement. But, said Kierkegaard, "They did not fly because the corn was good and the barnyard safe."

Ministering and teaching in urban centers *is* a risk. In many ways it is beyond the historical experience of our denomination, as it is with many denominations. But the people of the city are children of God. We can learn the language with which to teach them God's Good News, and together we can fly. As Abraham went forth in faith, he took enormous risks. Are we willing to risk?

Persevering by Faith

The second thing we learn from the Hebrews account of Abraham's story is how he persevered by faith. Abraham really lived by the promise of God. Earlier in the chapter the writer of Hebrews tells us, "Faith is the assurance of things hoped for, the conviction of things not yet seen." Reading the story in Genesis very carefully, we find that Abraham never really possessed the Promised Land in the way that we think of ownership. When Sarah died, Abraham went to the Hittites to *buy* land for her burial. Yet we affirm that Abraham "received" the Promised Land. It would be more accurate to say that Abraham possessed the Promised Land by faith—knowing that the time would come when God's promise would be fulfilled completely and his descendants would have full possession.

The Lesson of Faith and Hope

We, too, are called to live by faith. As we look at the problems in cities—violence, crime, unemployment—we are called to live in the faith that God's kingdom, depicted as a city, is a source of hope for us today. The hope of God's coming kingdom empowers us to be the body of Christ in the cities of today. We are called to live by faith that cities now will ultimately be transformed by the coming kingdom of God. Hebrews 13:14 says, "For here we have no lasting city, but we seek the city which is to come." The city which is to come empowers us to work for the welfare of cities today.

Is it just possible that as we work for the welfare of our cities we will find our own welfare? In Jeremiah 29:7, the prophet writes to the Jewish people who have been defeated, subjugated, and exiled to Babylon around 587 B.C. It is a devastating time for Israel. The city of Jerusalem, even the Temple, has been leveled and left in ruins, and its leaders carried off. Knowing of their deep pain, Jeremiah writes and tells the Israelites, "Seek the welfare (shalom) of the city to which I have sent you, and pray to the Lord on its behalf, for in its welfare (shalom), you will find your welfare (shalom)." Even though Babylon was regarded as the enemy, as evil and defiled, Jeremiah calls on the people of God to infuse the city with shalom, not to form a community apart from the city. Only as they sought the well-being of the city would they find their own well-being. Though despair was all around them, they were encouraged to live by faith and hope. And they were called to roll up their sleeves because of that hope.

Faith and hope point toward the future, and the future of the church in the city depends upon its religious education in a large way. Against the odds, in spite of the obstacles we can, with God's help, persevere in faith and be the body of Christ in the cities of today. Our commitment to the ministries of faith and hope, including religious education in the city, will bear fruit in kind.

As Abraham persevered in faith and hope, so did the Babylonian exiles to whom Jeremiah wrote. The Church of the Brethren is challenged to persevere in the same hope and faith as we travel toward the city.

Modeling the Kingdom

The third meaning in this story of Abraham is to live in a way that models the kingdom, or in the words of Hebrews 11:16, we are to live in a way that God is not ashamed to be called our God. The writer says our forebears who lived by faith were like strangers and exiles on this earth seeking a homeland. Because they lived by faith, verse 16 says, "Therefore God is not ashamed to be called their God for he has prepared for them a city."

Shortly before my husband, Peter, and I moved to the Indianapolis Northview congregation in 1978, the church was visited by Tom Wilson, a black who at that time served on the Elgin staff. The neighborhood around Northview had experienced traumatic "white flight" in the early 1970s. In less than two years the neighborhood went from being all white to being 60 percent black. Realtors walked up and down the blocks encouraging white homeowners to sell their homes quickly before they lost all their value. In the midst of this chaotic time, Northview, like many churches, did little. Members of the church perceived themselves as neutral. They said blacks were welcome to attend, but they hadn't done anything to actively encourage them.

When Tom Wilson arrived early one summer evening for a meeting with the Church Board, he sat in the church parking lot with his car window down. A young black girl—maybe four years old—peddled up beside him on her Big Wheels. "What are you doing, mister?" she asked. Tom responded that he was waiting for some other people to arrive so they could go inside for a meeting. "Oh mister," she said as she looked up at his black skin, "this church isn't for you."

Is God ever ashamed to be called our God? Is God ashamed of unwillingness to reach beyond white, Anglo-Saxon heritage to people who are not "just like us"? Is God ever ashamed that our denomination is mostly made up of middle-class folks—that few of our congregations include really poor people? Is God ever ashamed when we behave so differently than the kingdom is supposed to be?

Haven't we heard it said that the church should be a model of what the kingdom will be like? People should be able to look at our congregations and see a reflection of God's kingdom. The church, like the kingdom, should be a place of which God doesn't have to be ashamed. It should be a place where people see kingdom-like love, justice, caring, and compassion.

Children and other earnest learners keep us remarkably honest by unerringly pointing out our inconsistencies. The rewards of a commitment to urban religious education is that we will be led by those whom we teach to live up to our teachings. We will learn to model the kingdom, because nothing short of that will work. So God will use learners and teachers, preachers and servers to build congregations of whom God is proud, in whom can be glimpsed the kingdom.

Glimpses of the Kingdom

Now and then as I visit some of the Churches of the Brethren in the city I get glimpses of the kingdom.

I glimpsed the kingdom when I saw the Brooklyn Church of the Brethren filled with Hispanic children and teens. This church, formerly white and Italian, is located in an impoverished, inner-city area, heavily populated with drug dealers and prostitutes. Families in the neighborhood are poor; many of them work as domestic help. Most of the youth never graduate from high school. But now, a dozen or so of those young adults are in college because pastors Earl and Phill not only gave them a vision of going on to college, but they typed application forms for them, helped them find scholarship grants and loans, helped them believe that it was possible. Coming from families with barely enough to eat, these kids now have new hope and opportunities. In years to come, these young adults will be strong, capable leaders in the Church of the Brethren.

When I sat in the Brooklyn Church recently, I heard the children's choir of thirty or so Hispanic kids sing exuberantly about their faith. I found tears running down my cheeks. I listened to testimonies from members about what the church meant to them. One young man, now a pre-med student, said that the pastors had been like parents to him. Regularly he had eaten at their table; weekly they had done his laundry. Another man told how he had been cared for by the church when he was in prison. Church members also had visited his wife and had given money. He was released a few years ago, and his family has been active in the church ever since. He said it is now the most important force in his life. Seeing lives touched by the Brooklyn Church, I glimpsed something of the kingdom.

I glimpsed the kingdom at Miami First. Ten years ago the church was nearly ready to close—only a handful of whites still hung on in a community that had changed around them. They had tried to halt vandalism of the building with additional bolts and padlocks, a forbidding fence around the property and a locked gate at the driveway. When Bill Bosler came as pastor in 1976 it was on the condition they would open up the building and property and themselves, that they would in the words of Luke 9, "Lose their lives in order to find them." They reached out to new people, and in so doing the congregation is now made up of Puerto Ricans, Nicaraguans, blacks, Salvadoreans, and whites. The church has grown both in numbers and spiritual commitment—a glimpse, I believe, of the kingdom.

I glimpsed the kingdom in the Washington, D.C., City Church of the Brethren where the members run a soup kitchen. As many as 150-175 hungry persons are fed each day. Members from a number of rural Churches of the Brethren help by bringing truck loads of fresh produce into the soup kitchen.

I glimpsed the kingdom in churches where they have learned that other cultures, other nationalities and backgrounds bring enrichment to our lives. Merle Crouse told me of a black woman from our denomination who said a number of years ago, "I bring the heritage of Africa, of slavery, of my own dear slave grandmother. I join all that heritage of the black experience with the Brethren tradition so that the Brethren tradition is added to and enriched. Now my history is your history; and your history becomes mine. All of it is now our heritage."

When the church faithfully models what the kingdom of God will look like, then God has no reason to be ashamed to be called our God.

CONCLUSION

In summary, the story of Abraham and the Promised Land in Hebrews 11 challenges us:

First, to risk;

Second, to live by faith and hope; and

Third, to live in a way that models the kingdom so that God is not ashamed.

The Abraham story informs us that as we seek to be obedient to Christ's command to go into all of the world, that we will need to be more present in cities and that we will need to commit ourselves to urban ministry and urban religious education. We will need to learn, as a denomination, from the story of the cat and the mouse: "In order to survive, you gotta be bilingual." We will need to speak both the language of rural life and city life and use both languages to teach the gospel.

Like Abraham, the Church of the Brethren is called to sojourn in hope, toward the vision to which God invites us. Let us go forth in faith now—but let us broaden our path to include the population centers of today, as we travel toward the final, ultimate City of God.

Chapter 5

Christian Literacy, the Core Curriculum, and the Urban Church

Kay Kupper Berg

The urban church faces many issues in its religious education work that defy solution. A mere glance through this book reveals the diversity of the context, and even the definition of the urban church. For every point that urban churches have in common, another point can be named that makes them different from one another. Similarly, in a world of change and multiple options, where all churches feel the pull of societal diffusion, urban churches feel it earlier and more intensely. Often a combination of factors prevents churches from confidently focusing their energy and educating for Christian literacy. This chapter is about improving both by building a solid religious education program that is not only based on common essential beliefs and materials, but that also acknowledges and utilizes congregational differences. Urban churches can take the initiative in their own situations by developing a core curriculum that will be the strong center that equips Christians to live faithfully in a diverse world and that opens to all the gospel message of hope.

A core curriculum is, as its name implies, a set of materials based on a core of central beliefs. It is a set of essential teachings found in Bible, liturgy, hymnody, doctrine, and church tradition. These essential core teachings provide the foundation for the urban church's religious education programing and literacy in the Christian faith.

Precedents

Historical precedents for the core curriculum concept can be traced to the first century. Scholars believe that certain parts of the gospels came into being as the early church reflected upon those portions of the ministry of Jesus which were particularly important to teach. We have in the early accounts what is tantamount to a core curriculum of the acts and words of Jesus. The Didachē was a document of similar intent. Creeds and formalized confessions accomplished the same purposes. All of these set down in a teachable form the essentials of faith. Later on, the formal catechisms provided a firm central core or foundation upon which the larger religious education agendas were constructed. While we have moved away from rote memorization of questions and answers and shifted to the life-situation concept of curriculum in order to attain relevancy, the need for a well-known, well-digested central core of knowledge has once again arisen.

A core curriculum will most often be supplementary to another curriculum plan as essentials are brought before the students again and again as they move through other lessons. At times, the core curriculum will become *the* curriculum, expanded in ways appropriate to various age levels to insure a thorough learning. A core curriculum answers the new Christian's questions, "What is Christianity and membership in this church all about?" It answers the young person's question, "What does it mean to be a Christian?" It answers the congregation's question, "Who are we?" as times and circumstances change.

The Product and the Process

A congregation creates a core curriculum by indentifying a set of basics to be learned (scripture passages, creeds or statements of faith, liturgical sentences from the sacraments, hymns, prayers, details from church history, and the parish's cultural tradition). The suggestion that local churches take the initiative in defining essentials and putting together a religious education program is not meant to be revolutionary, but practical. The starting point is naming the essentials, and that start itself generates benefits.

In creating a core curriculum, both the process and the product are empowering. The very process of thinking through the core curriculum helps to focus the work of that church and give continuity. That exercise in clarity can be useful for the urban church by giving guidance to the religious education program as a whole and by helping to articulate the church's identity. In making the decisions necessary to establish a core curriculum, a parish reaffirms its roots. It identifies the ties of faith that it has with other Christian churches, and it also lifts up those qualities that make that congregation unique.

Similarly, the product outcome is beneficial. The product is not as confining as is a formal catechism, even though a catechism can be a central part of the core curriculum. Rather, the core curriculum serves as a foundation upon which new building can be done. Its intent is not to solidify the old and shut out the new but rather to preserve tradition while allowing new traditions to develop naturally. It need not be static, but it is the start and should be custom-made: "These things we believe. These things we cherish. This is what we will teach. This is who we are."

The Urban Church Need for a Core Curriculum

Urban churches have many characteristics that point to a need for a core curriculum. Although they share with other churches the perennial problems facing a religious education program, they bring to the situation their own particular sets of challenges. Like churches elsewhere, they must compete with all the distractions of the modern world that keep people from church school. Like other churches, they must conduct their programs within the limitations of irregular student attendance, limited parental support, and fluctuations of teaching and planning staff.

But some challenges are intensified in the urban setting. One is (scheduling.) Often urban churches draw parishioners from a wide geographic area, causing the church to consolidate its programing as much as possible. That often means that even more activities are crowded into an already full Sunday morning when attendance is highest. Sometimes religious education feels the squeeze. A core curriculum can help an urban church focus its attention and energies so that religious education time can be used to its fullest potential. It can free a church to use that time unapologetically because the church has defined its goals.

Another characteristic of urban churches that presents a challenge is mobility. People move to and from the city, and within the city from neighborhood to neighborhood and from church to church, bringing with them a plurality of prior experiences and backgrounds. In light of such patterns, a core curriculum can provide continuity by identifying shared essential beliefs and teachings and putting these in positions of emphasis. A core curriculum makes it possible to identify the knowledge needs of the newcomers and quickly involve them in study of the basics of the faith that they might easily miss.

The characteristic of diversity among urban churches poses another challenge to religious education programs. Frequently urban churches have difficulty finding curriculum resource materials that fit their needs. Although many excellent educational materials are produced at the national level, it is impractical for denominational publishers to develop curricula for unique situations. The materials that suit all churches suit none exactly. This is the case in both highly heterogeneous and highly homogeneous churches found in the urban setting. All urban religious educators adapt the materials they use to meet the variations of their particular situation, variations such as age grouping, attendance patterns, degree of family support, racial background, language and ethnic heritage, local social issues, preferred emphasis in the lessons, and so on. A core curriculum can help religious educators make these decisions. When a congregation defines the essentials that it wants in its religious education program, it can use that list as a guide when choosing from among published materials; it can use that list to tailor those materials to its specific needs; and it can use the list to articulate that church's curriculum desires to publishers who are interested, as most are, in making their materials more relevant.

CHRISTIAN ILLITERACY

A more pervasive and limiting situation that urban churches face is Christian illiteracy. This lack of basic vocabulary and teachings and traditions of the faith prevents people from fully participating in the life of the church and seriously hinders their faith development. Christian illiteracy can take various forms: not knowing key Bible stories, teachings, and verses; being unable to articulate what one believes; being unfamiliar with and therefore cut off from the liturgy of the church; not knowing hymns and prayers central to the traditions of the church and therefore not feeling fully a part of worship. Christian illiteracy is not merely an inconvenience or lack of conformity. It is a severe handicap that keeps people from hearing and celebrating and telling others the Good News.

Biblical Illiteracy

Evidence of Christian illiteracy is abundant, but a few examples will make the point. The first involves biblical illiteracy.

I was walking past our TV set one fall afternoon when I heard the announcer describe former Los Angeles Raider's quarterback, Jim Plunkett, as the "Lazarus of the NFL." Thinking that was a good modern metaphor, I shared it the next week with my freshman composition class at the community college where I teach. Their reaction surprised me. They knew who Jim Plunkett was, all right, but they failed to understand the metaphor because they thought Lazarus was a local department store. Later, I repeated the story to a young colleague on the faculty, thinking we could "tsk,tsk" together over it. But instead he said, "Refresh my memory. Who was Lazarus?"

In a literature class the next semester, we read Langston Hughes' short story, "On the Road," with its obvious allusion to Samson. Even after I drew the clear parallel between the character, Sargeant, and the Nazarite who pulled down the pillars of the Philistine arena, only one student in twenty-five knew who I was talking about. One might conclude that these students were simply unchurched, but even within the church there are many children and adults who do not know basic Bible stories and passages.

Doctrinal Illiteracy

Closely related to biblical illiteracy is doctrinal illiteracy, an inability to summarize succinctly the elemental beliefs of the faith. I overheard a discussion among junior high students in my church school class one Sunday. Someone at school had asked two of them the question, "Jesus was just a very good man, wasn't he?" While I thought it encouraging that eighth graders would be discussing theology in the cafeteria, I was disappointed to hear that my students had no answer to that challenging question. Statements of faith sprang immediately to my mind, but not to theirs: from the Apostle's Creed on the first page of the Evangelical Catechism: "I believe in Jesus Christ, his only begotten Son. . ."; from a memorized Bible verse: "For God so loved the world. . . "; from a favorite hymn: "Fairest Lord Jesus, Ruler of all nature. . . ." These children had grown up in the church but were not equipped with specific statements of faith upon which to draw when needed. They had learned nothing by heart and could not reply with confidence.

Liturgical Illiteracy

An example of liturgical illiteracy came to light in my own American Baptist church not long ago when it became apparent that certain programing decisions had inadvertently kept children from witnessing the Lord's Supper. We realized when the children presented themselves for baptism somewhere between the ages of thirteen and seventeen that, because they had left the sanctuary on Sunday mornings to go to church school classes midway through the service, most of them had seldom witnessed the sacraments. Even though they had been present occasionally, it had not been often enough for them to know that this rite was a basic and regular part of our worship. They had learned about it, but had not been part of it. It was easy enough to change our patterns so that our children became literate through regular observation of this important part of worship.

Christian illiteracy is more serious than the cultural illiteracy detailed by E.D. Hirsch[1] because the stakes are higher. As Christians called to be in the world but not of it, it is imperative that we know who we are. And it is imperative that that knowledge be made available to all. The Israelites brought Joseph's bones with them out of Egypt as a reminder of who they were and of what God had done for them. In the wilderness and in the land beyond, when they were beseiged by other gods and other options, the ark provided a center of focus. Generations later, on the road to Emmaus, Jesus enlightened two disciples by interpreting scripture to them: "Then he began with Moses and all the prophets, and explained to them the passages which referred to himself in every part of the scriptures" (Luke 24:27 NEB). Presumably, neither of the disciples said, "Moses who?" or "Lazarus who?" Their understanding of the moment and the future depended heavily on their knowledge of their past.

Benefits of Christian Literacy

The benefits of Christian literacy reach far beyond understanding an announcer's clever metaphor or not having to mumble and fake the words to a hymn. Christian literacy is the bond that links us with our past, unites us with other Christians in the present, and provides guideposts for the future. We want the benefits of Christian literacy and more for the next generation. But the bonding must begin early. We know that if Christians are to live lives grounded in the faith, the foundation stones must be there. The core will equip the students to learn the richness of the faith that will continually come before them in their lifelong growth toward full maturity.

As late twentieth-century Christians, we have extricated ourselves from some of the confining doctrine and narrow biblical interpretation of the past, but too often, instead of taking our ark with us, we have set it down and are wandering around in a theological wilderness out of sight of the promised land. We need to reclaim the ark. We need to name the Name, recite the certainties of our faith, testify to the changlessness of God in a universe of options. In other words, we need to teach the basics—simply, directly, consistently, energetically. A core curriculum can help us do that.

AN URBAN CHURCH EXAMPLE

One church that is making progress in the core curriculum concept came to the realization that the children and youth were missing out on some very valuable learnings even though the church school program was relatively well run and positively viewed. The church was a larger downtown church that experienced a moderate degree of mobility and moderate heterogeneity. Almost all of the education programing was concentrated on Sunday mornings week by week and a series of intense week-end retreats for youth spaced through the year.

Elementary School Age

The first thing this church did was adopt a supplementary curriculum for grades 1 through 6. A small booklet was prepared and shared with all teachers, students, and parents. It contained materials divided into four categories: Bible skills, stewardship, mission, and Bible content.

Bible skills include naming the books of the Bible, finding passages in the Bible, using Bible reference books, and learning about the Christian seasons of the year from a Bible perspective. Stewardship involves becoming familiar with the church's stewardship plan and action and having a chance to begin participating in various stewardship programs. Mission education focuses on national and world mission programs of the denomination and on various local mission projects in which students may share. Bible content involves the memorization of a list of passages judged by the planners to be of significance for participation in worship and for general basic knowledge of sections often referred to in teaching. The list includes the Lord's Prayer, Psalm 23, John 3:16, Psalm 100, Matthew 7:12, Matthew 22:36-40, 1 Corinthians 13, Psalm 121, 1 Corinthians 11:22-26, the Ten Commandments, the Beatitudes, and Matthew 28:19-20.

Other church lists will differ. Some will focus on verses central to a "plan of salvation." Others will have a different list of "favorite verses." Others will concentrate on learning parables and teachings. The list offered is not meant to be normative, but illustrative of the first steps toward a core curriculum taken by one church. The idea is that throughout the first six years of Sunday morning religious education, and to varying extents at home, these materials will be taught and retaught within and around the ongoing church school curriculum.

Junior and Senior High School Age

Having identified these essentials for grades 1 through 6, the church, through its Board of Christian Education, turned its attention to junior- and senior-high needs. At this level the church addressed the following challenge: "What is it that our youth should know before they graduate from high school in our church school program?" The goal was stated in this form: "To so teach and learn that our youth will be grounded in the Christian faith as seen in central biblical, historical, cultural, and ethical principles for the living of the Christian life. To this end, we will develop courses that are both intellectually as well as spiritually enriching, draw upon the best talent and teaching resources, actively involve youth, and expect the support of parents."

Committees met, conversations with youth were held, discussions with parents took place, examination of catechisms and similar materials from other traditions was undertaken until a consensus was reached about twelve courses that would constitute the core curriculum for youth. These would be taught on a three-year cycle, with room each year for student electives.

Junior-high courses include *The Life of Jesus—The Gospels*, which provides an overview of the life and ministry of Jesus as presented in the gospels. *The Book of Acts and the Mission of the Church* traces the movement of the early church from the gift of the Holy Spirit to the narrative exploring the movement of the church from Jerusalem to the Gentile world. *Leaders of the People of God* uses Old Testament characters to demonstrate how God can work through a leader by developing an individual relationship that would enable a life of decision making. *Comparative Religions* provides a basic exposure to some of the world's other major religions. *Our Baptist Heritage* traces the history of American Baptists and the local church. *The Psalms* introduces some representative samples from this timeless book of worship and praise.

Senior-high courses include *The Bible: Its History and Its Unity*, which examines the textual and structural unity of the Bible. *The Message of Jesus* focuses on the message of Jesus' statements about the kingdom of God and on his action toward people whom he encountered. *Moral and Ethical Decision Making* introduces some of the principal moral and ethical issues that Christians face in today's world and representative methods of making decisions about those issues. *Religion in American Life* traces some of the main developments in American religion from the beginnings of European exploration to the present day. *The Law and the Prophets* traces and highlights the emergence of the Hebrew nation from the Egyptian Exodus to the giving of the Law of Moses. *Cults* familiarizes students with cults in our country and examines the key beliefs of each.

This junior- and senior-high curriculum builds on the foundation of the ongoing teaching and on the Supplementary Curriculum of grades 1 through 6. It reflects both the essentials of the faith that this one church shares with other Christians and the particular emphasis that this congregation wants in its religious education program. The core curriculum was initiated by the church to fit its circumstances. The result is a focused, energetic religious education program and increased Christian literacy.

The precedents for a core curriculum are there. The need exists. The benefits are many, especially for the urban church. It is unlikely that core curriculum will be prepackaged at a national level in a manner that will fit the diversity of urban churches. But the concept presented here is within the reach of any congregation willing to take the time to reflect on personal experience and congregational patterns to uncover that core. Any congregation can use that core to teach the essentials of the faith that insure Christian literacy and a chance at full participation in the richness of the Christian life.

NOTES

1. E.D. Hirsch, *Cultural Literacy* (Boston: Houghton Mifflin, 1987).

Chapter 6

Spiritual Formation in Urban Church Education

C. Renee Rust

Spiritual formation, the process of nurturing persons in their personal religious lives, can help urban religious educators remove any alienation they feel toward the city, help them identify personally with the spiritual power of the city, and help them affirm the city and become empowered to work effectively in it. That energizing spiritual journey passes through six areas of focus. First, persons involved in urban religious education can recognize the dilemma of the mixed messages the Bible gives us concerning cities. Second, these individuals identify with the spiritual power of the city by imagining and meditating upon an "inner city" of their own creation. Third, they can examine the central role of law in the city and consider that relationship. Fourth, they can examine their own perspectives and humbly admit their own limitations. Fifth, they can learn from existing spiritual discipline models. And finally, they can celebrate the city and their part in it.

BIBLICAL CITIES: HOLY OR UNHOLY?

The first focus of spiritual formation for urban church education reveals a difficulty: the biblical tradition that at worst denigrates the city and at best displays ambivalence toward it. Stories of the destruction of Nineveh, Sodom, and Gomorrah leap to mind. Babylon, whose whoring ways image the evils opposed to God's plan, sharpens the dilemma. In spite of its holiness, even the Holy City of Zion was problematic due to its other-worldly character: Zion required divine transformation before it could become a place worthy of God. Augustine of Hippo reenforced that dualism by insisting on his parallel between the City of God and the City of Man, for by definition, parallels never meet. Deuteronomy 6:10-12 subtly underlines the disparity in Yahweh's message that the Chosen People are dissociated from the cities: They will arrive in prosperous towns not of their making.

On the other hand, it is the countryside that seems to be the chosen ground for divine-human encounters. Mosaic mountains and wildernesses far removed from the city were places for those meetings. Eden, where humans first enjoyed God's company, was a garden—not a metropolis. In Christian monasticism, the desert has epitomized the way to escape from a wicked Rome fraught with innumerable immoralities. By using themes of withdrawal to find The Holy, pastoral images beckon Christians to the monasteries and renewal centers—in effect away from populated sites—to be alone with The Alone so that one may become All One. Even if these images are not understood literally, they underscore the threat of temptations lying in wait to prowl upon unsuspecting Christians in their cities (see Psalms 59:6 and 1 Peter 5:8-9).

However, there are *some* Hebrew and Christian scriptures depicting goodness in the city. Jerusalem's dependency upon God to relieve her unhappiness is a positive quality in Isaiah 54:11-12 and Lamentations 1:1ff. and 4:1,5. Ezekiel affirms a connection between the city and God's presence by asserting the city's future name: Yahweh-Is-There (Exodus 48:35). When the city of Sodom was destroyed, the plains got equal treatment (Genesis 19:23-24). In the Book of Revelations, at least seven cities have enough merit to receive angelic attention. If cities are no good, why does Hebrews 11:16 speak of God's preparing a city for the faithful?

Whoever scans the gospels will find that an itinerant Jesus addresses crowds more often in the towns than on the hillsides:

Caesarea, Nazareth, Jerusalem. The Samaritan woman rouses the citizens of Sychar to come forth to hear this amazing fellow (John 4:28-30). Paul the Apostle depends upon populated centers to spread the Good News: Rome, Corinth, Ephesus, Phillipi, Thessalonica, Colossus. In the Acts of the Apostles, sites of gospel action are named Troas, Miletus, Damascus, Gaza, Jaffa.

A starting point in spiritual formation for urban religious education is meditation upon Judaeo-Christian scriptures which relate the city to divine goodness. This is a way to deal with a possible sense of alienation from the life of the city.[1]

The cities of the Bible, as the cities of today, appear to be neither good nor bad in and of themselves. But as centers of human life they are arenas for God's word and salvation.

YOU WERE CALLED TO BE THAT CITY

The second focus of spiritual formation for urban ministry is personal identification with the spiritual power of the city. Here is an exercise to help: Individuals and groups can reflect on various selected aspects of their own and others' spiritual journeys in symbolic terms. In the model provided below, questions one through eight invite solitary reflection in preparation for sharing responses around the final three questions designated as "Describe," "Tell," and "Decree."

FACILITATOR:

"One way we can take a journey is by using our memory and imagination. We can explore a city of our imagining, our own personal inner city.

"By the time we were twelve (and since that time) the foundations for our present personal inner city have been laid. As we come to reflect on the questions below we may come to understand the city of God within, the kingdom. We will be invited after a period of solitary reflection (about one half hour) to voice some of our responses with others in the context of a faith sharing group.

"The use of the city as a symbol will allow individuals the freedom to reveal whatever they wish and to conceal what they wish to keep private."

In the city of my imagining:

1. Where do my city limits start? Where do they end?

2. How fast has my city grown, and who or what has helped it grow?

3. Where are the parks, schools, cathedrals, hospitals, and jails in my city?

    a. What space does school occupy in my city's development?

    b. Where are the parks in my town, and what are they like?

    c. Where are the cathedrals located (at what points in time and circumstances in my journey)?

    d. How and where do I see the hospitals in my city?

    e. Do jails have a place in my inner city?

4. Do I have any one-way or dead end streets?

5. Have there been different kinds of homes in my neighborhood?

6. How does the cemetery fit into my city?

7. If someone took a tour of my inner city, what points of interest would I want to highlight for that person (points he or she shouldn't miss)?

8. What kind of city do I find in myself overall, (e.g., a village, town, metropolis, farming town, one-horse town, etc.)?

Guides for Faith Sharing in Groups

Describe: What is the kind of key that would open the gate of your city (to God's presence)?

Tell: What blocks or locks the city gate (to the Lord and to fellow human beings)?

Decree: What is required to enhance or develop the sacredness of your city?

A group of seven or eight including the facilitator is ideal. The facilitator explains that whatever each person says in response to the three preceding areas is to be received in reverent silence. Each person will be given the opportunity to present his or her approach to each of the three areas above, without argument or discussion.

It is important that the facilitator be the first to share his or her answers to the "Describe," "Tell," and "Decree" questions.

After a person has completed all three areas, the facilitator invites others to respond by reflecting to the speaker what he or she as a listening member has heard. Each responder attempts, in addition, to affirm the witness of the speaker even if it is by a simple "Thank you for sharing your faith (or your personal journey)."

After all have had opportunity to respond to the sharer, the facilitator moves the group on to direct their attention to another member, and the process repeats until all have finished.

A short prayer or biblical text by the facilitator brings the faith sharing to a close. Or if feasible, a closing prayer is sung or said in common (e.g., the doxology) is appropriate.

NOTE:

For groups that desire a more direct application of the preceding exercise, members gather again after a brief break to discuss:

a) How they perceive the sacredness of existing cities.

b) How the church(es) can enhance the spiritual potential of actual cities.

c) What they themselves are willing to offer to the service of city dwellers.[2]

LAW: SHEDDING LIGHT ON THE CITY

The third focus of spiritual formation for urban religious education examines the central role of law in the city. As centers of population, cities are shaped by and are shapers of law. Just laws delineate the ideal, protect the rights of individuals and groups, and echo the justice intended by God. Thus one generalized route for seeing the city's holiness is to examine the relationship between cities and law. We first must alert ourselves to the pros and cons of some disparate understandings of urban life. Becoming aware of the role of law in organizing and maintaining people's lives together is a way to demonstrate the distinct attitude involved.

Consider the city as an organic matrix of human life. No matter how many ethnic groups, cultures, or lifestyles are represented, the city itself supersedes all these individual parts. A town's natural virtue lies in its ability to be ecumenical, that is, to embrace in one house, so to speak, the complex diversity it invites. In this way the city has the capacity of doing what Christians claim the gospel does, namely, to bring about peace and good will among peoples based on something other than comfortable similarities. A metropolis minimizes similarity by fostering diversity and making it work so that "our city has a lot to offer." Thus it attracts more diversity and works hard at making it work for all concerned.

The task is this—to bring to conscious understanding what it is that makes the city work and to do so by considering three distinct attitudes in Christian tradition in respect to the role of law. Discerning the assumptions about the function of the law reveals how the city and humanity itself are valued. This kind of reflection grounds the urban religious education in a vision of what is ultimately valuable.

THREE ENLIGHTENING POSITIONS

A summary of three Christian stances toward uses of the law includes first, the Pauline view: Law orients us toward the ideal. This precept of course does not hold that the city is good in and of itself but that it needs law to point it toward its future worth. In this way law functions to highlight the dualism between one's sense of the city as less than fine. It implies the need for the Augustinian City of God.

A second view of law is that it is an organizer of civic life. Citizens are already deserving of a harmonious existence. This view implies that urban life is good enough on its own, so good in fact that the gathering of the people deserves the structural supports provided by just laws. A corollary is that law has no virtue on its own unless it is promoting human life to the fullest degree possible.

John Calvin proposed a third view of the law by making it the prerogative of Christians. In this framework law is divinely ordained. Christians are the ordained ones elected to live their special lifestyle and thereby to sanctify the city. By implication, civic life is unworthy on its own without the benefit of the righteous elect who redeem it.

Calvin accepted the first two uses of the law summarized above but added his third dimension. Along with Calvin, the

Roman Catholic Church incorporates all three. Martin Luther accepted the first two but rejected Calvin's perception.

Because of its universal appeal, the second view, while seeming the most radical, is also the most promising for promoting the basic goodness of the city as a human matrix. It is the view undergirding international law by which not only cities but nations can live in peace if not in harmony. The second position implies a trust in people just as the Constitution of the United States does to be able to provide a life of realistic coexistence according to common sense, vis a' vis, agreement on the basics for survival and development.

Endorsing the second position calls for practical application. It calls for a program of spiritual formation that requires an intentional experiential immersion in urban life to stimulate a sense of its wholesomeness. It may seem strange to realize that it is possible to be in a city and yet remain unaware of those who live in the city in all of its dimensions. In the service of the life of the actual inhabitants of a given city we can help ourselves to interiorize positive valuations of the city as a vital experience of the human community we seek to serve in the name of Jesus. The agenda is dear to the God of the Bible whose characteristic willingness to participate in human life respects the nature of that life and encourages renewal from within.

This conscious and reflected-upon experiential component of urban living is a *sine qua non* for spiritual formation. The first level of participation is becoming a sensitive city dweller by pitching the ministerial tent in the midst of the city with as much affirmation as possible.

TO MAKE GOOD VERSUS TO MAKE BETTER

The fourth focus of spiritual formation for urban ministries involves self-assessment. Following from affirmation of urban life via biblical references, personal identification with the city, and discussion, those who live in the midst of the city, citizens need to focus not on how to make the city good but how to make it better. To understand oneself as a servant to the city rather than a savior of it demands an asceticism which abstains from righteousness. No one in urban religious education culti-vates effectiveness more by becoming a student of the city than a teacher of all those who are and have been getting along quite well without that religious education work.

In other words, those in urban church education must first find out what makes the city simultaneously so appealing and so frightening to throngs of people. Churched dwellers face surprising lessons from the marketplace about what it takes to make life more attractive via architecture, human traffic, sights and sounds, variety, order among disorders, the interchange among business people. The risk lies in the probability that the city might teach the churches realities that are different from our expectations. Admittedly the city has its seamy side. The goodness already throbbing through it can always be bettered by someone's standards. But when we recognize the less-than-desirable aspects of the city, we can then discern what form of involvement we can engage in as Christ's representatives in Christ's pattern to stimulate the growth of just and peaceful urban life. When we put aside our preconceived notions about what is "good" for the city and instead look and listen to the existing good and find ways to make that better, then we will be channeling our energy in the right direction.

SPIRITUAL DISCIPLINES FOR INTERACTION

The fifth focus of spiritual formation for those involved in urban religious education is to learn from existing spiritual dis-cipline models. Two spiritual traditions which seek to work hand-in-hand with the surrounding culture instead of negating or merely preserving it are the Rule of St. Benedict and the Yokefellow philosophy. The Benedictine strain is over 1500 years old. The Yokefellows date from the 1940s.

Benedict of Nursia was inspired by evangelical hospitality, which overtook his earlier withdrawal from wicked Rome. The fundamental attitude of hospitality welcomes all forms of life as guests in the monastery or, today, on our planet. Thus this classical Western spirituality supplies a strong flavor of the ecu-menical interface exemplified in city dwelling. A more contem-porary version of Benedictine spirituality emerges in the Anglican Coventry Discipline and its extension into the community of the Cross of Nails, which is committed to the mission of reconciliation. Reconciliation is the acid test of hospitality to the stranger and perceived alien. The more recent Yokefellows, seeded in Elton Trueblood's early writings, are more specialized in directing their efforts precisely into the realm of civic life.[3]

Both Benedictine and Yokefellow spiritualities ask participants to reflect on their experiences and to grow personally as they synthesize them. Spirituality never exists as a generic reality. It must always be concretized, personalized, and realized action-reflection. Pertinent tools for reflection include: dialogue with another person or group who can appreciate one's context of faith, recording personal reflections in a journal/notebook, meditation, and prayer. An individual needs to process learnings in light of experience from time to time to become more intentional about his or her personal contributions to the life of the city. Spiritual disciplines can provide the inner resources from which to draw energy.

THANKSGIVING IN ACTION

The final focus of spiritual formation in the urban setting is a natural outgrowth of the other five. Exploring and examining urban goodness, participating in the urban matrix, and personalizing one's commitment to the civic enterprise will lead to celebration. A program in spiritual formation will help people in urban ministries to find appropriate, explicit, communal modes of celebration. In churched circles this usually takes the form of communal prayer/liturgy/worship or some related ritual event. We enter into prayer in order to place our lives explicitly in the realm of a greater reality. Shared ritual accents the larger realm both in motive and in consequence. Hope for a larger reality calls one into prayer, and Christian worship draws us right back into the hope that we can offer ourselves a larger spirit of generosity to one another. A similar dynamic is at work in celebrating the life of the city through communal rituals.

One way to celebrate or appreciate the city is to enter into its ritual moments of greatness. As in a small town the annual

Fourth of July parade often promotes this appreciation, so in a large city like New York the St. Patrick's Day parade confirms the larger realm. In May and November, civic rituals call for becoming informed about campaigners and voting for those who appear able to help create measures serving the larger common good as public figures. A celebration of and in the city means taking part wholeheartedly in cheering the baseball team because of its excellent performance and sharable glory.

At times, we will be exhilarated by carrying out a more private progressive prayer with chosen friends in a downtown area. Moving from the highway to the square to a walk in the night, aware of the city's mystery, we use psalms or psalm excerpts to mark our path. Even a few people can effectively and unobtrusively exult in the wonder of the city without grandiose concepts imposed by either church ceremonies or civic rituals. A final example of embracing the city's rituals is the church that hosts a meeting of urban planners or a group of small business personnel intent on creating local jobs.

People working with one who is engaged in a spiritual journey will find in such a place a larger reality than apparent at first glance. For they will meet a minister whose spiritual formation has prepared for weekday collaboration in addition to Sunday service, both oriented toward upbuilding the human community dear to God's incarnate heart. Spiritual formation puts those involved in urban religious education in touch with God's redeeming power. It allows them to recognize, affirm, and celebrate the goodness of the city and to find energy and expression to work with urban dwellers to make the city more like the holy city of God.

> There is a stream whose runlets gladden
>   the city of God,
>   the holy dwelling of the Most High.
> God is in its midst; it shall not be
>   disturbed;
>   God will help it at the bread of dawn.
> The most High is with us;
>   our stronghold is the God of Israel
>   Psalm 46:5-6,8[4]

Chapter 7

A History of Religious Education in the Black Church

Colleen Birchett

We begin our examination of the history of religious education among black people in the United States by going to the
earliest recorded instances. Quite clearly the black church was
not an urban church in the beginning, nor is it exclusively an
urban church today. But the urban black church can only be
understood by looking at the nonurban beginnings as well at
the various urban influences that have come along in the years
between then and now.

Slavery
    The earliest record of religious education among the slaves
was in 1619. However, pre-1619 observations were document-
ed by American students, missionaries, and various travelers.
Such people noted that black slaves during this period believed
in a Supreme Being, but believed that God made the world and
left it. There were still residuals of many African religions, such
as the belief in disembodied spirits and fatalism.[1]
    During this period there were many reasons that English-
American Christians did not want to teach the slaves about
Christ. For one thing, according to British law it was illegal for
one Christian to hold another Christian as a slave. If a slave
became a Christian, that slave would have to become a free

man or woman. Therefore, religious education of slaves was prohibited by most states. There was also the unsettled question of whether blacks had souls.

Spanish and French colonies did not have the same laws regarding the enslavement of one Christian by another. In fact, Spanish settlers were ordered by the king of Spain to teach religion to slaves and the French "Code Noir" said that masters must enlighten slaves in the principles of the Christian religion. During this period also, Catholics were teaching religion to some slaves.

Eventually the English resolved their moral dilemma by declaring that conversion to Christianity does not necessarily mean freedom for a slave. New laws were passed in English colonies saying that conversion does not bring freedom—a new interpretation of scripture. This change paved the way for slavemasters and others to offer religious education to blacks in a more organized way.

The Eighteenth Century

During the early 1700s, one of the few efforts to provide religious education for slaves in America was that of the Society for the Propagation of the Gospel. This society was established in London in 1701 to work among blacks and Indians in the colonies.[2] As part of the Church of England, it sent a number of clergymen to evangelize the slaves and to provide them with basic religious education. These clergymen included Samuel Thomas (1702), LeJeau (1706), Ludan (1717), Gilbert Jones (1711), and Parnal (1722), whose parish had as many as 700 slaves, some of whom understood English.

However, in the main, the white settlers were not very concerned about the religious education of the Negro, saying that Negroes were too stubborn to become real Christians, that they were too wicked, and that owners could not spare the time for them to take the classes. There was widespread hostility against the Church of England. However, the Society for the Propagation of the Gospel continued to fight for the religious education of blacks, and it became the single most significant agency for the religious activity of Negroes in the South. In 1783, however, the Society's operations had to cease due to the separation of the United States from England.

During the latter half of the eighteenth century there were some efforts among white Christian denominations to educate slaves, but most such activities were handled by various missionary societies. In 1738, Moravian and United Brethren began to establish such missions exclusively for blacks in the South, but with very little success. These societies left the South altogether due to the societies' favorable attitudes toward the antislavery movement.

The Presbyterians, in Virginia in 1747, made some efforts to instruct blacks. Two clergymen, Samuel Davies and John Todd reported ministering to 300 and baptizing them. Methodists sent missionaries south from New York in 1769. Their efforts were first confined to New York, but after the revolution, in 1786, they moved into the South and reported as many as 890 members of one church and 11,680 conversions by 1790.

Baptists throughout this period were also evangelizing and instructing slaves. However, in the main there really was very little teaching of slaves during the eighteenth century. Most activity, outside of special small-scale organized efforts, was carried out by isolated white ministers, some Christian slaveowners, and occasional missionaries. Therefore the great majority of the slaves during reconstruction were not reached via any formal Christian education program.

The development of religious education programs was retarded by questions related to how to treat black slaves within white church congregations. Should slaves be subordinate within the white church? Should a separate Negro church be formed? In the end, both systems were adopted.

However, as other separate churches were adopted, they came under attack by Abolitionists. In response, some states began to pass laws to prohibit assembling of blacks for religious purposes. These laws made it mandatory for blacks to attend white churches. Religious education of blacks was tightly controlled, and was largely confined to Sunday morning preaching, which they listened to from balconies of the churches.

Missionaries who attempted to take religious education of blacks beyond Sunday morning preaching were viewed with hostility and suspicion and frequently were denied access to

blacks. This may have been the beginning of the conceptualization, within the black culture, that religious education takes
place primarily through the medium of preaching, on Sunday
morning, and is confined to the Bible as the medium of instruction. Residuals of this notion are prevalent among black church
members of today and remain one of the issues that need to be
addressed by any modern religious education program.

However, participants of the Great Revival in 1790 broke
through these barriers, and Presbyterians, Methodists, and Baptists began to evangelize and instruct blacks in large numbers,
through camp meetings. During this period 4-5,000 blacks
were baptized. In addition, congregations of blacks began to
emerge.

The Nineteenth Century

What almost brought a halt to instruction of blacks was reaction by southern whites to the Nat Turner rebellion. White
southerners blamed the Abolitionists and others and made it a
crime for blacks to learn to read or to congregate for religious
purposes or religious instruction. These laws were passed
throughout the South (South Carolina, 1834; Missouri, 1817;
Virginia, 1819; Louisana, 1830; Georgia, 1831; Mississippi, 1831;
Alabama, 1832; North Carolina, 1835). This resulted in a stagna-
tion in Christian education for blacks. The only education offered during this time was education by isolated white ministers and slavemasters. The content of this instruction was designed to support the docility of slaves.

Throughout this period, however, isolated white Christian
voices cried out against neglect of religious education for
slaves. Richard Freeman, president of the State Baptist Convention of South Carolina, issued a pamphlet. Rev. Dalcho of the
Episcopal Church of Charlottesville, Virginia, also issued a pamphlet. The Agricultural Society of South Carolina, holding its
annual meeting in 1829, also cried out against the conditions of
education among the slaves. As a result, there was again a
gradual increase in interest in the religious education of slaves.

While it was still illegal for Negroes to congregate separate
from whites during the latter half of the nineteenth century, this
did not prevent various white religious groups and free blacks

from vigorous religious education activities and programs. This was done through local churches and missionaries societies. The Methodist-sponsored Freedman's Aid Societies in Boston, New York, and Philadelphia sent northern teachers to the South to educate blacks. In addition, the Freedman's Bureau in 1865 established a total of 4,239 schools in the South with a total of 9,307 teachers and 247,333 students.

The Freedman's Bureau schools were not necessarily religious schools, but by helping blacks to learn to read they opened the way for them to learn to read their Bibles. This cooperation between religious and secular education was underscored by the fact that the Freedman's schools were sometimes held within the confines of churches throughout the period of Reconstruction and during the post-Reconstruction era.

Plantation missionaries also sprang up during the period just prior to Emancipation. In 1837, the Society for the Religious Education of Negroes was founded in Liberty County, Georgia. Black church memberships grew to as many as 11,546. Methodists had 26 missionary stations, employing 32 preachers, and the Southern Methodist Episcopal Church also reported having 172 missionary stations with 145 missionaries.

During its thirty-four years of slave missions, the Methodist church reported paying 2 million dollars for the evangelizing of the slaves; 200,000 black slaves were reported converted. The Protestant Episcopal Church, which began missionary work in 1821, organized separate congregations for blacks. Missions were established in Charleston, Raleigh, Petersburgh, and in a few other places.

With the laws against separate black churches, blacks were usually confined for their religious education to balconies of white churches. They were under direct supervision of white churches and instruction was through the medium of preaching on Sunday morning.

After Emancipation

After Emancipation, blacks left white churches and established their own churches. By 1906, 36,770 black church organizations were in existence in the United States. Of that number 90 percent were located in the South, and they had a total membership in the neighborhood of 3,685,097. There were 4,779 Sunday schools with 210,148 teachers and officers in charge of 1,740,009 students. Since 1890, then, the black population had increased 26.1 percent, but the church organizations had increased 56.1 percent and church edifices had increased to 47.9 percent. The value of church property among blacks had increased by 112.7 percent.

The Early Twentieth Century

As the black church moved into the twentieth century, one of the greatest problems it faced was uneducated clergymen. Only 1 percent of rural clergymen had any theological training and only 3 to 5 percent had as much as a high school education. In the cities, only about 5 percent had any training at all. These clergymen continued to magnify the importance of preaching, but deemphasized the importance of teaching and teacher training agencies within the church. Moreover, as new church edifices were constructed, they were designed to facilitate preaching, with sanctuaries but without classrooms designed for other types of instructional activities. Teachers and other agents of the church were not formally prepared for their work. There was in black churches a general lack of vision for the educational mission of the church. There were widespread inadequate buildings and equipment for the Sunday schools and other training auxiliaries.

All of this was despite the fact that, in the early twentieth century, black churches brought in an income of 86 million dollars annually—about $2,100 per church. There was about one church per 255-260 people, with an average membership of 116 per church.

Even larger congregations, however, did not see the need to incorporate facilities for Christian education. According to Sims, Leland, and other researchers, emotion worked against the development of an educational plan. Most churches had a Sunday school, but few were adequately administered or organized to give any notion of what the Sunday school should be. Ministers, in the main, saw Sunday school as a distraction—not as a resource.

A survey of 609 black churches' religious education programs in 1933 revealed one-department schools with all age-groups grouped together, one general superintendent, and a set of officers. Few black professionals were working in the church (5 percent of the Sunday school teachers were professional school teachers, 3 percent were physicians, but 92 percent were housewives and untrained laborers). There was also a general weakness in young people's work. There were few if any young people's societies and very little self-expression of youth. There were almost no weekday religious schools. However, the black church was the center of community life.

A black church culture evolved without the benefit of a formal, more-structured religious education program in the modern sense. With the exception of Sunday school (seen primarily for the education of children), most black laity received their only formal Christian education directly from the pulpit. A small minority of each church also attended weekday Adult Bible Studies.

National Religious Organizations

After Emancipation, a number of national black religious organizations were formed. Examples include the African Methodist Episcopal, the National Baptist Convention, and others. Moreover, black churches belonged to some of the large white denominations. However, membership, for the most part, was in name only, with very few churches actually participating in the educational activities of these organizations.

The survey conducted by Sims in 1926, revealed that 90 percent of these nation-wide denominations had published standards for organization and administration of the Sunday school. Fifty to 70 percent fostered young people's associations and unions and other societies which were to meet weekly (such as BTU). However, there were no prescribed courses during the early twentieth century. Sixty to 80 percent promoted missionary societies within churches, in which study courses and Bible study courses would be offered to local congregations. Such courses, in the main, were offered by the denominations, but were rarely replicated in local churches. Local leaders did not encourage this work. There was also a general lack of black-oriented print materials.

Black Seminaries and Foreign Missions

While there was a general lack of interest in the religious education of black laity, there was a strong interest in educating black ministers and in funding the evangelism of blacks in foreign lands. The pattern was to support Home Missions and to establish religious seminaries to train black ministers. Black churches of the South contributed as much as $250,000 annually for Home Mission work.

There were also large contributions to foreign evangelism. The National Baptist Convention (1916) had sixteen Home Missionaries, and $17,000,000 was contributed to foreign missions in South Africa, South America, and the West Indies. The National Baptist Convention established 110 schools and contributed $220,000 to their support. The African Methodist Episcopal Church established Wilberforce, Payne, and Turner Seminaries and a number of smaller schools and colleges. The African Methodist Episcopal Zion Church established five colleges and academies. The Christian Methodist Episcopal Church established five colleges and lower schools. By 1926, black churches owned and supported 153 schools (60 large and influential, 93 small and less important). Attendance at these schools was in the range of 17,299.

These schools were primarily for training clergymen and teachers. The teachers were trained to teach basic education skills. Because several states had passed laws prohibiting black and white students from converging in the same educational institutions, those black ministers who were trained for the ministry were trained at all-black colleges such as Morehouse, Virginia Union, Bishop, Shaw, and Tuskegee. Persons other than ministers who attended these schools went to get other kinds of vocational skills. However, these schools were not generally used to train black church laity to carry out functions specific to the black church.

Moreover, historians have focused on the curriculum of these early efforts to train black ministers, noting that the religious education was handled by untrained volunteers from organizations such as the Young Men's Christian Association, the Young Women's Christian Association, Student Volunteers Movement, representatives of young people's societies of various denominations, and temperance societies.

Leland's research reveals that these general conditions did not really change much between 1890 and 1960. Although seminaries and colleges existed, by 1960, only one out of fifteen black ministers had attended seminary training. Most who had, had attended unaccredited institutes and Bible schools. Most pastors of the South had no exposure to accredited seminaries. Moreover, other researchers noted that there was very little effort by large white denominations to intentionally develop black ministers.[3]

Research on Religious Education and the Black Church

All of the early historical patterns cited in the immediately preceding paragraphs continued, for the most part, to the 1960s. With the civil rights movement there was a gradual increase in the availability of formal education to black ministers, and to black people as a whole. However, there has been very little research documenting whether the general improvement in education resulted in an improvement in Christian education programs in black churches as a whole.

A computerized data base search revealed that, while there has been a proliferation of research studies on the black church in general, very few studies have focused on black religious education programs in particular. The studies which have, have focused on one particular program or another, pointing out the successes or failures of the program. Many of the programs studied were church-based tutorial programs designed to provide basic education skills to young people.[4] A few doctoral dissertations focused on particular black church-based religious education programs and approaches.[5] A large percentage of the studies located were historical studies of the black church or of black church religious education programs at various historical periods.

Only two statistical analyses of black religious education programs could be located. The first was done by Scripture Press[6] and the second was done by Thomas Leland as a dissertation for Southern Baptist Theological Seminary.[7] In both cases, the researchers sent out questionnaires to black churches from mailing lists that they had compiled from various sources. Scripture Press sent out 5,110 questionnaires and got back 195

(3.8 percent response rate). Leland sent out 347 and got back 66 (19 percent response rate). In both cases, the researchers felt that, while the number of respondents was low, the respondents were representative of black American churches.

The results of both surveys tend to suggest that since the 1960s there may have been a dramatic increase in religious education programs in black churches. There may also have been a dramatic increase in the educational preparation of black pastors. In the Scripture Press study, for example, 61.3 percent of the black churches responding to the survey had Boards of Christian Education (compared to 65.3 percent of white churches answering a similar survey). More black pastors than white pastors reported spending most of their time in an average week in sermon preparation than in any one of five other pastoral tasks. Out of seventeen educational needs, black pastors ranked highest in priority "better trained laymen." In 1970, 5.4 percent of the black churches had full-time salaried directors of religious education (compared to 7.1 percent of white churches). The desire for better-trained black laymen tended to increase with the size of the Sunday school:

100 or less	35.7 percent
101-250	36.4
251 or more	45.5

Leland found that of the 66 churches responding, 41 (62.1 percent) had Boards of Christian Education. A full 100 pecent had Sunday schools, 90 percent had Vacation Bible Schools and 56 (84.8 percent) had training hours. Both the Scripture Press study in 1970, and Leland's study in 1981 found black pastors as perhaps the main agent of instruction, with 52 percent of the Scripture Press respondents saying that they offered pastors' instruction classes, and with 83.3 percent of Leland's respondents saying that they offered pastors' instruction classes.

Scripture Press found the most popular education agencies in black churches to be Sunday school, youth fellowship or training hour, and Vacation Bible School. About two-thirds of the black pastors expressed the need in Sunday school literature for more relevance to student interests and expressed the need for more pictures and photos of persons of other racial groups than white American. There was also an indication of generally greater interest in the development of youth, with black pastors saying that they needed special material for high school and college career classes.

It appears that, by 1970, a much higher priority was being placed on church-based religious education programs. However, the results of the study do reflect some of the historical trends identified in the immediately preceding paragraphs.

The Need for Black-Oriented Leadership Training Materials

Leland noted that most large denominations today express the need for Christian education materials for blacks. These include Episcopalians, Church of God, and Disciples of Christ. Moreover, most of the large black denominations have publishing houses which have published some black-oriented training materials. Urban Ministries also distributes black-oriented materials to local churches. However, in the main, this literature has focused primarily on Sunday school, Vacation Bible School, and (as is the case with the National Baptist Convention), Bible Study material for the Baptist Training Union. Some nationally known Christian religious educators have written books on topics of interest to the black church and to black Christian families. However, to date, most training materials outside of Sunday school materials, have focused on aids for sermon preparation. Materials that have been produced, in the main, have not been produced within the structure of a comprehensive curriculum design. While religious education theorists such as Olivia Pearl Stokes[8] advocate developing a national curriculum of leadership training materials designed for black churches, no such curriculum has been developed by black church organizations. Moreover, large white denominations continue to this day to hesitate to develop such materials. This is due to several unanswered and still controversial questions:

Is the white leadership really committed to a program of religious education for the black church?

Isn't the material currently being produced for the white church adequate? Wouldn't merely adding pictures of blacks suffice?

Should the approach be monoethnic or multiethnic?

Can one model curriculum be developed for various settings?

How will such materials be marketed?[9]

Summary
History can teach many things which can be used to plan the future for religious education programs in black churches. One thing the past has taught is that the black church is both resilient and strong. It has been very creative during the various stages and forms of racial oppression. In the midst of Jim Crow laws, discrimination and segregation barring participation in some of the leading theological seminaries of the country, the black church evolved solutions. It built its own black seminaries. It created educational institutions to provide blacks with basic educational skills. It evolved a religious education program which was delivered directly and almost exclusively via the pulpit. It also became the central institution in black community life.

However, for half of the twentieth century, the black church did not really build adequate religious education programs outside of black preaching. During the latter half of the century, with the onset of civil rights legislation and increased opportunities for the education of blacks, there seems to have been an increase in church-based educational programs. As the Scripture Press research suggests, by 1970, black pastors were beginning to express the need for new types of resources, and the need for "better trained church laity." More than half had created church-based Boards of Christian Education.

All of this says that the black church is now ready to meet new challenges. As the summary of the Urban Ministries Needs Assessment suggests (Appendix I), the relationship among religious education, evangelism, and special church ministries is beginning to be understood. The harvest may be ripe for new leadership training products that are black-urban oriented.

NOTES

1. See Charles Sims, *The Religious Education of the Southern Negroes* (Louisville: Scripture Press Foundation, Christian Education Re-

search Division, 1926) for information and data regarding the early history of blacks in the South and religious education as developed in this article.

2. See Thomas Elgon Leland, *Developing a Model of Religious Education for Black Southern Baptist Churches* (Louisville: Southern Baptist Theological Seminary, 1981).

3. See James S. Thomas, "The Intentional Development of Black Ministry," *Occasional Papers* 29, December 2, 1979 (Nashville: United Methodist Church, 1979).

4. See Maurice J. Esch, *A Comprehensive Curriculum Evaluation of the Christian Action Ministry Academy in 1970* (Chicago: Illinois University, 1970) and James P. Comer et al., "The Summer Study-Skills Program: A Case for Structure," *The Journal of Negro Education* 38:1 (Winter, 1969).

5. Walter Henry McKelvey, "A Study of a Developing Cooperative Christian Education Project in a Cluster of Black Churches in the Triad Region of the Western North Carolina Conference of the United Methodist Church" (Madison: N.J. Drew University, 1983). William Gerald Howard, "The Adult Bible Study Group as a Potential Education Change Agent in the Black Church" (Madison, N.J.: Drew University, 1982).

6. Scripture Press Foundation, "Report on Christians in Black Churches" (Chicago: Scripture Press, 1970).

7. Leland, *Developing a Model of Religious Education.*

8. Olivia Pearl Stokes, "The Black Perspective: Christian Education in Today's Church," in *To You Who Teach in the Black Church*, ed. Riggins R.Earl Jr. (Nashville: National Baptist Publishing Board, 1972). For a full-blown and superb treatment of the black vision and perspective on religious education, see Olivia Pearl Stokes, "Black Theology: A Challenge to Religious Education," in *Religious Education and Theology*, ed. Norma H. Thompson (Birmingham, Ala.: Religious Education Press, 1982), pp. 71-99

9. Leland, *Developing a Model of Religious Education.*

Chapter 8

Learning to Face Diversity in Urban Churches

Robert E. Jones

I believe that the greatest challenge facing the local church in urban metropolitan areas is the summons to move beyond racial, cultural, and socioeconomic division toward being multicultural, multiracial congregations. I believe this is an educational, pastoral, and theological challenge, a challenge called for by the gospel. After all, the gospel focuses on the building of a visible presence of the kingdom of God. I believe that an intentional, planned education and leadership program must be initiated by the churches. Such a program should exemplify and focus on building and maintaining multiracial and multicultural churches, in order for the visible presence of the kingdom of God to exist and flourish.

For the church of Jesus Christ not to become this reality in a multiracial and multicultural world is to ignore the gospel's call to seek to be reflective of this existence, and is to disregard the truth and purpose of God's creation. Both black and white churches, as well as any other homogeneous churches in the urban metropolitan area, must take the challenge to become racially, socioeconomically, and culturally inclusive, intentionally, as a command of God as revealed and taught by Jesus Christ in the gospel.

While there exist in the life of the church many valid struggles of different types toward becoming more inclusive, I have selected to focus on the church's struggle with being racially inclusive. To be sure, the church needs to work on becoming more inclusive of women, of people of different religious and theological perspectives, of socioeconomic status, and of those with disabilities. Notwithstanding, it is my contention that failure to become racially inclusive is more divisive and devastating to the churches than failure to be inclusive in the areas mentioned in the preceding sentence. Some persons might argue that it is more difficult to attain socioeconomic inclusivity than racial inclusivity. I question that argument on the basis that anyone can change one's socioeconomic status by financial attainment and professional achievement. This is not the case for persons who are ethnically born. If you are black, you are black; if you are white, you are white; if you are Oriental or Hispanic, you are Oriental or Hispanic.

What Is the Lesson Our Churches Now Teach?

Walter Ziegenhals speaks in this vein and quotes other writers with whom he agrees.

> The racism rampant in the churches plagues the vitality of Christianity in today's urban setting. . . . Racism is a fundamental denial of the church's task to regard all persons as brothers and sisters and to reestablish community in places of suffering. . . . The most conspicuous fact of life in the city is racial division. It may be equally true to say that the most conspicuous factor facing the church in a racially transitional or pretransitional community is that of its own racism. The white racist attitude of church people constitutes a critical component of the problem.[1]

Can We Teach What We Are Not?

The question for religious educators is: Can we teach what we are not? Can we teach about the love of God surrounding and making a people one when we live in our churches in these excluding patterns?

Based on my own interpretation of scripture, I believe that there are too many Christians who regard the racial and cultural homogeneity of the local church as the way things are and ought to be. This is one reason why so little has been done to develop and maintain local congregations that are racially and

culturally inclusive. There are many church growth theoreticians who say that the fastest growing and most stable churches
are those that are homogeneous. I question whether growing
fast into a large homogeneous church means that the church is
also authentically faithful and genuinely Christian. If we are
ever to move beyond the separation and division that exist in
the life of the local church, leadership, planning, and resources
are required at all levels of the church. Resources are available
and the context is available, but priority for using the resources
to support and maintain the development of multiracial, multicultural churches is scarce and inadequate!

The Segregated Church Denies the Lesson of Diversity

The prophetic words of Martin Luther King that "the eleventh
hour on Sunday morning is the most racially segregated
hour of the week," point to a serious hypocrisy in the life of the
church. Let me call attention to several interesting facts about
the struggle for desegregation of our society and the nature of
pluralism in the life of the church.

The church, especially the mainline denominations, both
black and white, have been in the forefront of the struggle
calling for justice and equality for blacks and others that have
been labeled minorities. Church bodies, especially at the denominational level, have called out for voting rights and the
desegregation of schools, places of employment, housing, ho-
tels, motels, and restaurants as a moral issue. Churches have
worked to see that laws enforced these rights at all levels of
society. Because of these activities and the efforts of civil rights
groups, racial desegregation has become a reality in most levels
of our society, except in major positions of power and decision
making *and* in the local church.

Virtually all mainline Protestant churches, as well as Catholi-
cism, especially at the denominational level, lift up and celebrate what they call diversity and pluralism in the life of the
church. When one takes a closer look, however, one will find
little or no attention being given to local churches to develop
and maintain multiracial and multicultural congregations where
they exist or could and should exist.

One of the problems is that there is no agreement in black or white churches that a multiracial, multicultural church is a great asset that should be fostered. There are many black pastors who call on denominational executives to work for the development of ethnic churches and not for integrated ones. There is the feeling among many black pastors that integration is bad for the black church, the black community, and black people.

A St. Petersburg, Florida, newspaper quotes the point of view of Henry Lyons, pastor of Bethel Metropolitan Baptist Church: "I don't favor segregation. What I favor is survival—survival for black people. I'm not anti-integration. I'm just pro-black. I want blacks to love each other more, to spend more time with each other. The church is the only thing the black man does control. If he's going to forsake that—good God almighty—he's not interested in his identity. I see no hope for blacks if that happens."[2]

Lyons rejects the argument that blacks who live in integrated neighborhoods such as Lakewood, would attend white churches if black churches are farther away: "What's a few miles for your dignity? What's a few miles for your heritage? What's a few miles to see a black in a position you can respect? It's an outright betrayal, especially by the so-called black middle class."[3]
dle class."[3]

There are little or no leadership monies or resources designated for multiracial, multicultural churches. Some people argue that multiracial, multicultural congregations are not viable and stable congregations in our day. They say the only places where multiracial, multicultural congregations exist are those which are in transition. It seems unreasonable to those who argue this way to designate and allocate resources for unstable churches in unstable neighborhoods. How can the church teach about a God who cares for those in trouble and is present to those in turmoil when there is an apparent general belief at all levels of the church that the viable congregation is the homogeneous congregation? A quote from a self-study of May, 1975, of the Pacific Presbytery shows the type of alternative that some churches consider: "Should we not, instead of attempting to save (white) congregations in the process of racial change, recognize that there comes a time when the best thing to do is to close the church or merge it with another in a nearby area and begin again in the area to organize a new (black) church?"[4]

The History of this Condition

The lack of local church initiative and effort to become multiracial and multicultural is the primary reason for the scarcity of such congregations. The creation and development of the black church was the result of the white church's refusal to accept blacks in their congregation as equally worthwhile children of God. When blacks in the late 1700s found that whites were not willing to accept them in worship services as equals, they left the white churches and created their own where they could worship God freely. Because the black worship experience, from its inception, has always combined the worship of God with the struggle against powerful whites who oppress them, members of white churches have always found it uncomfortable and difficult to identify and relate to the black worship experience. Most white church members who are ill at ease with the black religious worship style also assume that blacks will be uncomfortable and unwilling to relate to white religious styles. This attitude resulted in few, if any, invitations being extended by white church members to blacks to join them in worship.

Blacks have their reasons for not inviting themselves to white churches or inviting whites into black churches. Blacks have more than three hundred years of history as evidence that whites do not want to accept them as equals. The black church is the last place where blacks are not forced to confront racism. The black church is the only major institution left in the black community that is totally owned and operated for and by black people. Black institutions which have been integrated have suffered the loss of black identity and control and have been subjected to a new form of racism.

The teaching that comes through the life of the church is that worship must be comfortable. Thus members of both white and black churches perceive the homogeneity of worship as being comfortable and easier to handle than the struggle with prejudices of blacks and the racism of whites. This attitude must be put aside if authentic worship is to take place, and there seems to be little hope that the church can teach in the classroom any valid lesson about the equality of all when the congregational identities teach otherwise.

It will be interesting to see how the black church will deal with the growing number of young whites who are now moving back in black communities in the city. It is a new day, as James Davis and Woodie White say: "It has been said that, for too long, integration has been a one-way street—the movement of black to white institutions and white churches. Now the churches may be given the opportunity to provide a more comprehensive definition of the integrated church."[5]

Prejudice and Institutional Racism in the Life of the Church

There is a general consensus among black sociologists that while prejudice prevents blacks from naturally joining with whites in white congregations, it is the racism of whites that prevents the change in structure which would permit and encourage integrated congregations. The way racism is defined requires that racists have power. To be a racist one must not only be prejudiced, but one must have the power to enforce and perpetuate one's prejudice on others and then do so. For this reason, the argument is made that in our society it is impossible for blacks to be racists, not because they are incapable of having biases and prejudices, but because of their lack of power to forcefully practice their prejudices against another race or people. But within the homogeneous black church, blacks have the power, and therefore the potential to be racist.

The Place for Homogeneity

While heterogeneous congregations are being developed, some homogeneous elements must exist in these congregations.

These will help:

1. Agreement between whites and blacks that a particular denominational polity is acceptable and beneficial to their mutual participation as members of the body of Christ, as evidenced by a common interest in improving neighborhoods, schools, and community.
2. Common interest in moral and social justice issues, as well

as in faith and community issues, as means of promoting better understanding, respect, and trust.
3. Ability to celebrate together the pluralism in one's denomination as evidenced in the truth of Paul's words to the early Christians: "For as many of you as were baptized into Christ have put on Christ. There is neither Jew nor Greek, there is neither slave nor free, there is neither male nor female, for you are all one in Christ Jesus" (Galatians 3:27,28).

When local congregations are able to move beyond racial and cultural differences to a point where on any given Sunday—not just on Race Relations Sunday—their congregational composition is multiracial and multicultural, then a major step toward God's kingdom will have been taken. Then the church will teach by its composition as well as its verbalizations the fullness of the power of the gospel to bring all together at the foot of the cross.

How Can We Move Toward the Rainbow Church?

I maintain that the ideal setting for the development of multiracial and multicultural churches is twofold: a transitional community and transitional churches within a pluralistic denomination. There will always be churches within a pluralistic denomination. There will always be churches in transition, so there will always be an opportunity to develop multiracial, multicultural congregations. After World War II, whites en masse began to move out of the city to the suburbs. For their part, blacks and other minorities began moving into the city. Now that whites are beginning to return to the cities it will be interesting to see how black churches handle their new white neighbors. I know of no better way to reflect and proclaim and teach our belief that all people are created in God's image than by demonstrating this in our life together in a way that shows we respect each other and treat each other as equals. White churches must move beyond feeling and acting on the premise that keeping things the way they are is best for all concerned. Black Christians must move beyond feeling and acting on the premise that the black church and the black congregation should maintain their black composition in order to preserve their ethnicity and to provide a haven from the racism that exists in society and the world.

This is not to suggest that a multiracial, multicultural church must be a congregation in which people do not lift up and celebrate their ethnicity and cultural differences. Nor am I suggesting that such a congregation be one in which persons do not see racial and cultural differences when they are together. To say, "I do not see differences" when differences exist is to fail to see the distinctiveness of God's creation. The genuine multiracial, multicultural church is one in which differences are seen and recognized as challenges as gifts for one's faith and obedience to share in each other's differences and become one family in Christ!

Christians, black and white, must come to realize that together rather than separately they can better achieve security and control and promote the kingdom of God on earth. There is every good reason to teach not only that which we have in common but also the specific and fullness of the separate heritages that we bring to the multiracial and multicultural urban congregation.

In the church and in society today, there are two ways in which prejudice and racism are manifested: either in a brutally overt manner, as seen in South Africa, or covertly as it is institutionalized. While the former needs no explanation, the latter is seen as a systematic prejudice which oppresses people for the purpose and goal of achieving social ends. In the institutionalized white church it works in ways that bring Jonah to mind.

Jonah and the Contemporary Church

First, the church does not want to accept the challenge of ministering and witnessing to minority peoples whom they think are unworthy and have little to share or offer to God; who will not meet expectations; upon whom time and resources will, perhaps, be wasted. Like the biblical Jonah they decide to move away. Walter Ziegenhals notes that "the central cities of the great metropolitan areas of the United States are rapidly becoming home for black and Latino peoples."[6]

Fear Reigns

Second, the institutionalized church permits fear to influence the decision not to accept the challenge of ministering and witnessing to city people. It fears that to live in the city is to fraternize with death and destruction. To Jonah, the Ninevites were wicked and wanted to kill the prophet rather than to receive him and God's message.

God Might Act in a Strange Way

Third, today's institutionalized church feels that God may do something strange like offer love and mercy to minority people of the city. Like Jonah, these people do not want God's benefits shared with unworthy people. Like Jonah, too, many people today have a love-hate relationship with the city: a love for its benefits and a hatred for those aspects that are considered negative, including the people who live there.

The Loss of the Church

A fourth consideration is the totality of those problems, issues, and struggles of humanity which threaten the institutionalized church's very existence. In running away from the city, the church loses its distinct and significant power to impact the world and society for God and God's kingdom. Mainline denominational churches are losing thousands of members and have closed hundreds of local churches because of inability to witness effectively to society. Isn't there a marked resemblance to Jonah ending up in the unexpected haven of a whale's belly? For church or prophet to gamble with God is to lose.

A Future Salvation

The fifth and last of our Jonah likeness looks to the future. The church today can save itself if it will move beyond prejudice and racism to sharing the gospel with all, especially those now rejected by the church and society. This movement can bring salvation to all, because cooperation among people of different races and cultures is a means of establishing a stronger power base on which to build a better understanding of each other. The church must begin by dismantling its structure and institutional racism and proceed to replace these negative qualities with antiracist and antiprejudice structures.

This accomplished, the church can deal with the heart of the matter: racism born in and thriving on the economics of our society and our world. Prejudice and racism can and will be

dealt with most effectively by a more just and equitable distribution of wealth and power among peoples.

In an unwitting manner, the church teaches the story of Jonah in its patterns of avoidance and flight from the urban setting. How can there not be those who learn and relearn that
lesson? If we are to teach otherwise, we must become something that we have not yet become.

THE HOW-TO OF A MULTIRACIAL AND
MULTICULTURAL CONGREGATION: A CASE STUDY

For the past ten years I have served as a clergyman of a
thriving, growing multiracial, multicultural congregation. When
I think about the beginnings of this congregation, I am immediately reminded of a passage in the book of Exodus (14:14)
where it reads, "And Moses said to the people, 'Fear not, stand
firm and see the salvation of the Lord, which he will work for
you today; for the Egyptians whom you see today you shall
never see again.' "

A Decision

In 1970, this congregation with which I work made a drastic
decision that started it on its way to becoming the multiracial,
multicultural congregation that it is today. The congregation,
after having grown to 600 active members, began in the 1960s
to decline in membership. This was the result of the changing
racial make-up of the neighborhood in which it was located.
Many whites began to move out as blacks moved in.

In January, 1980, the congregation met and voted on whether
to remain in the present location or move west following the
white members who were moving out. The elders and pastor of
the church came to the congregational meeting recommending
that the congregation move, but the congregation defeated the
recommendation by four votes. All the elders and the pastor
resigned. Those who made the decision that the congregation
should remain and in fact did remain must have heard an echo
of the words of Moses, into which they substituted one word:
"Fear not, stand firm and see the salvation of the Lord which
he will work for you today, for the [problem] that you see today,

you will never see again." With new leadership emerging from
their adult Bible class and the assistance of the regional denominational office, those who remained were able to keep the
church going and moving. The new church leadership decided
that to develop a congregation reflective of the neighborhood
composition was not only important but necessary. This deliberate decision and the commitment to abide by it were most important to enable the church to move successfully in the direction of
becoming what it is today.

New Leadership
The second major step along the way was to find and develop black and white pastoral and officer leadership. It was important to demonstrate to the congregation and the neighborhood the sincerity of this commitment by showing willingness
to share positions of power regardless of race. When I joined
the staff as one of its bi-racial pastors in 1977 the congregation
had already achieved approximately 10 percent minority membership. At that point, the community was 39 percent black. As
of 1987 this congregation's racial make-up was 50 percent
black, 47 percent white, 3 percent Oriental, and 1 percent
Hispanic. This church composition is reflective of the present
composition of the neighborhood. Church leadership has continued to seek, to have, and to maintain an ongoing integrated
leadership—black, white, male, and female at all levels of the
congregation.

Finding qualified black and white leadership was not an easy
task. This was due, not to a lack of qualified persons, but to
dearth of qualified persons who were willing to commit themselves to work in a multiracial, multicultural church. I have
observed that it is not easy for pastors to move to other
churches after working and serving in a multiracial church.
Ziegenhals calls attention to the problem when he considers
the reasoning of both white and black pastors, and that of
ecclesiastical bureaucrats, as well as the question proposed by
some thinkers as to whether or not the institutions we are
describing ought, in fact, to survive. We listen to his words:
"White pastors would rather not serve them because in the
words of one, 'There is no longevity to a pastorate in racially

changing communities.' Black pastors prefer serving 'established' churches, where they can find a measure of financial and vocational security. Church bureaucrats look upon them as institutions to be pitied or scorned, a drain on the denominational dollar, a headache for the hierarchy."[7]

Teaching Ourselves about Fear

For our multiracial, multicultural congregation to develop, the words of Moses continued to echo, "Fear not, stand firm, and see the salvation of the Lord, which he will work today." There was surely the challenge of dealing with fears. First there was the fear that with so few people we might not be able to become a kind of church we ought to be in order to survive. Another fear was related to the neighborhood, namely, whether we could survive in a neighborhood that was racially mixed and changing. But the belief that when we are small and weak, God in Christ will make us strong was validated biblically and pragmatically. It is easier to become a multiracial, multicultural church in the setting of the small congregation than in a large one.

The Advantages of the Small Church

First: To develop and maintain a multiracial, multicultural congregation, many changes must be made. Changes often cause conflicts. Being small is more helpful and productive in situations where the majority of the people concerned are involved in the process in bringing the change about. There is more resistance to change when people are forced to face change without their consent.

Second: A genuine atmosphere of acceptance is necessary for a multiracial, multicultural congregation to develop and be maintained. People of different racial and cultural persuasions need to feel genuinely accepted into a new and different situation. It is much easier for the genuineness of this accepting atmosphere to be expressed and felt in small congregations than in large ones.

Third: In developing multiracial, multicultural churches there must be a sense of ownership. This requires participants to be directly involved in all facets of the life of the church. In small congregations, the survival of the congregation depends upon committed involvement of parishioners. The small church is ideal for creating a sense of ownership. There, efforts to be accepting, inclusive, and committed to qualifying fellowship can more easily and effectively be demonstrated. This in itself facilitates the attraction and ability to develop and maintain multiracial, multicultural congregations. If there is any place where one can see whether pluralism really works in the church, it can truly be seen in small congregations.

This is not to suggest that the large churches with two hundred or more members cannot or should not work toward becoming racially and culturally inclusive. I suggest that the large church can facilitate this process by organizing itself so that the conditions that naturally exist in the small church are fostered in the large church setting. It is desirable also to take seriously the challenge of becoming more racially and culturally inclusive. This will mean that the large church, because of its setting and structure, must work more diligently at creating an atmosphere of acceptance, ownership, and belonging.

The Place of Conflict

Conflict is a way of life for multiracial, multicultural churches and we were not excepted. Conflict was a method by which people were brought to the point of dealing with differences. Conflict stimulated creative energy which became the basis of working toward unity.

Authors Davis and White say that most churches become paralyzed by using a great deal of their energy trying to avoid conflict rather than facing it and working to allow it to become a creative and inventive tool for bringing about change and growth. They say that the avoidance of conflicts makes for what they call a "stalled congregation." The reason given why churches, especially churches in transition, respond this way are these: "They are afraid and bewildered. They may fear that if the conflict ever surfaced, they would not be able to handle it. The attitude that 'Christians don't argue' has prevented many congregations from gaining experience in successfully dealing with emotionally charged disagreements. In their already weakened condition, they may be afraid of losing members or strength needed for survival."[8]

Resistance Appears After a Good Start

As the church population progressively moved toward becoming 50 percent black, more blacks became excited about the congregation and invited new persons, both black and white, to become members. On the other hand, white members seemed to become more anxious and uncomfortable about the growing percentage of blacks. Enthusiasm on the part of older white members seemed to wane. Consequently, both older blacks and older whites seemed no longer to invite friends to consider belonging to the church.

What can this experience of mine, presented here as a case study for reflection, teach us about the process by which the multiracial and multicultural church comes into existence and becomes the setting where teaching and living can be congruent? It brings to mind these lessons:

Leadership: Lay and Clergy

One lesson is that there must be appropriate, qualified leadership at the congregational level. Persons in leadership positions must be committed to bringing about equality among all peoples within society and within one's particular church. The leadership of the local church must see as one primary task the development of its own congregation as a model for what the reign of love, equality, and justice is like. The leadership must have a biblical, theological basis and understanding undergirding its efforts. While a genuine compassion for people is of great importance, skill in being able to motivate and move people to greater openness and to new experiences is essential.

Critical to success is the religious education agenda of the local leadership. Leadership training at the seminary and at the denominational and local church levels teaches people, clergy and laity, how to understand and master these skills. Leaders must be trained to motivate local congregations to become more heterogeneous in their manner of living. The development of multiracial, multicultural churches will be severely hampered by the lack of qualified leadership in these areas.

Worship

The style and form of worship is the next most important lesson. What happens in worship will determine, to a great extent, the way the congregation will develop. Worship is a time of learning as well as celebration. Very seldom, if at all, will one find a local church that has been able to truly integrate into its own worship style and tradition, the worship style and tradition of other cultures. Black churches and other ethnic churches which include the style and traditions of white forms of worship are exceptional. When blacks or other ethnic people begin moving into white churches, they are received on the basis of their willingness to accept the existing style of worship as being normative. In most cases whether a white church becomes multiracial or multicultural is determined by the willingness of the incoming minority group to accept and participate in the existing worship style of the church. Several aspects of worship are focal points.

There should be a less-formal high church style and form of worship, one open and accepting to a mixture and blending of different cultures and traditions. Flexibility and openness are essential. This atmosphere can be fostered and nurtured by allowing as much lay and family participation in the worship service as possible. Having an informal announcement time, having Bible reading and prayers be led by persons of the congregation—these are means of creating an atmosphere of openness and acceptance of all people, regardless of who they are.

There should be diversity in music. This is another element of worship that helps to generate a sense of openness. To include in worship music of different styles and traditions of the various ethnic groups and cultures in your congregation is important. Of all the elements of worship, music is among the most sensitive. If one can develop diversity in music and in the style and form of celebrating baptism and the Lord's Supper, the congregation can and will move rapidly and effectively toward more openness to various cultures and races of people.

Efforts should be made to structure the worship service so that no one need feel that he or she is a stranger in a strange setting. Single persons, persons of different ethnic and cultural backgrounds, youth, children, all should be able to find something in a given worship service with which they can identify and find a sense of spiritual nurture and comfort.

A designated time for fellowship and the recognition of visitors is another lesson element. In many cases, the worship service is the primary contact where outsiders learn about the nature of the congregation. It is therefore an important time for informal conversation that permits visitors an opportunity to get to know people within the church and for people within the church to know the visitors. A time for the introduction of visitors during the worship may not always be the best avenue for introductions. Having a time for this purpose during fellowship hour immediately following the service is helpful in creating a better sense of companionship.

Education

Educational opportunities are another concern since deliberate efforts to promote fellowship aside from the time of worship are important. Leaders in a viable church work to develop relationships among diverse groups in ways and settings other than those provided on Sunday mornings. The best means of doing this is to give people opportunities to learn through experiencing differences and similarities.

Religious education resources and programs are aids in accomplishing our purpose. Since adults, as well as children and youth, learn from what they see, hear, feel, and touch, using such resources and programs as are acceptable to the group is another way to promote an atmosphere of congeniality. It is more important that resources and programs demonstrate a blending of diversities than that they focus on differences. However, it is better to know and recognize differences than to ignore them.

Outreach

The area of outreach mission is another place where we can help create sustaining bonds between people of diverse backgrounds. The secret of success in this activity is to find and present projects that provide the greatest degree of consensus. As people work together on issues of love, justice, and equality divisive walls and barriers disintegrate, and the workers tend to state implicitly their affirmation of each other. This builds stronger bonds among the collaborators and gives witness to observers that a wholesome spirit of harmony and friendliness prevails.

Teaching What We Are

The thesis that we cannot teach what we are not, stated in the positive, calls for us to be the lesson. As we learn to truly celebrate in a church where there is a balance of members' cultural involvement, languages, and so on, we can help each different group hold on to its identity. Such a church has a profoundly relevant lesson to teach to our world, for congregations that are mixed racially and culturally proclaim dramatically Paul's words to the Corinthians: "Therefore, if anyone is in Christ, he [or she] is a new creation; the old has passed away. Behold the new has come" (2 Corinthians 5:17). Racially and culturally mixed churches teach by their life that reconciliation with one another can follow from reconciliation with God. One does become a new creation, a new person.

What the church must work to achieve as a symbol of God's kingdom is unity with diversity. When people who differ work together and dialogue with each other about their differences and experience each other's differences in community, a new and exciting life experience emerges. This is the way we become truly a new creation in Christ, and that is the way we go forth and teach to make disciples of one Lord, one faith, one baptism.

All Christians are called to the ministry of reconciliation and we must be about it. We must find ways to deepen our reconciliation with God and with one another. More than teaching about it theoretically and theologically, we should be living it practically. If the church is to maintain its significant role in our society, people of all races and cultures must learn to co-exist in the congregation as they do in the work place and market place.

It has often been said that where there is life there is hope.

795 1

Can it not also be said that where there is hope and effort there can be accomplishment. The church can become the lesson of God's redeeming grace. The church can teach by its life the healing of the Lord. What then is taught in the classroom, or for that matter what is proclaimed from the pulpit, will have the authenticity of life as its authority. We can learn to be what God has called us to be, and we can then teach as he has commanded by our walk together into the world.

Notes

1. Walter E. Ziegenhals, *Urban Churches in Transition* (New York/ Philadelphia: Pilgrim, 1978), p. 28.
2. *St. Petersburg Times*, August 16, 1986, p. 1 B.
3. Ibid.
4. James H. Davis and Woodie W. White, *Racial Transition in the Church* (Nashville: Abingdon, 1980), p. 78.
5. Ibid., p. 95.
6. Ziegenhals, *Urban Churches in Transition* p. 94.
7. Ibid., p. 120.
8. Davis and White, *Racial Transition in the Church*, p. 75.

Chapter 9

Making the Dream Come True: Discipleship for All God's People in the Urban Church

Captolia D. Newbern

"Go therefore and make disciples of all nations, baptizing them in the name of the Father and of the Son and of the Holy Spirit, teaching them to observe all that I have commanded you, and lo, I am with you always, to the close of the age" (Matthew 28:19-20).

THE CHURCH'S MISSION TO TEACH

Religious education is a process of developing persons mentally, spiritually, and morally by teaching and experience and ministry. The acts of service which are geared to make disciples for Jesus to the glory of God, depend on the church being a community of redeemed people, "the body of Christ," as Paul describes it (1 Corinthians 12:12), whose foundation is Jesus Christ (1 Corinthians 3:11). The critically important dimension of this is the local church, the congregation, which teaches well or poorly by its whole life.

The charter of the church's salvation is "one Lord, one faith, one baptism, one God and Father of us all, who is above all and through all and in all" (Ephesians 4:5-6). The one holy food she partakes is the "bread and wine" symbolic of Jesus' broken body and the blood shed to save her. As God's gift to the world, the church belongs to *all* people, for language, race, "skin color," gender, vocation, calling, social status, locality, incident of birth and place, economic holdings, educational achievements, honors, political party, or religious heritage make no difference.

Today that church faces the stern test of ministering in the complex and sometimes hostile urban environment. The church faces, as never before, a set of temptations to worship false gods among a people turned aside from the true worship. The people are being taught the idolatries of this world. Can we teach them a true faith and a true worship?

A primary test of the church *is* its worship. It shall not worship objects, material possessions, or human creatures, but only God. The mission of the church is the mission of our risen Lord (Luke 4:19-21), and the eternal task of the church is to teach the gospel of Jesus. The role of the church is to demonstrate tangibly in its own life the worldwide unity that cuts across and transcends *all* barriers of cultures, historic traditions, heritages, and achievements.

The church is the church, whether it is in town, country, village, rural area, or city, but I speak primarily to the urban church in this chapter. The church functions in its total life of leadership and membership as co-partners, clergy and laity, share responsibility in all the ministries. Education is of prime importance because only a well-grounded church will survive the tensions of urban life. The very nature of the Great Commission commits the church to teach all that Jesus has commanded. Pronouncements come from on-high, but the religious education tasks of the church which I discuss here must be taken up and carried out by the church next to the people, the congregation and parish.

WHAT SHALL WE TEACH?

In urban religious education ministry, substantive program components are varied, numerous, and essential. I share here some basic principles that continue to prove fruitful in my professional ecumenical religious education activity at the grassroots level. I do so in the hope that they will be helpful to clergy and lay leaders and workers involved in religious education activity. They are phrased in questions as in a catechism.

Who Am I?

The fundamental dignity and worth of each person, regardless of condition of birth or ethnic affiliation, is rooted in his or her being in the image of God. From birth there lies ahead a path of self-discovery and spiritual understanding. The flower that grows from seed to its full bloom and "the earth (that) produces of itself first the blade, then the ear, then the full grain in the ear" (Mark 4:28) symbolize what happens as we gradually progress and learn who we are.

On this journey the voices of the city are quick to tell us who we are. Problems and periods of discouragement and difficult obstacles confront us. We cannot hope to hear an inner voice of identity in the clamor of today in an easily learned lesson for, as the prophet Isaiah instructs us, we progress in our understanding gradually, "For it is precept upon precept, precept upon precept, line upon line, line upon line, here a little, there a little."

As God's children of the earth, we are a part of this vast design. We unfold in accord with the pattern God, the Almighty. We teach in the presence of the local church in the face-to-face relationships that we are spiritual beings, children of an all-wise and merciful Creator; that we are his instruments of God-givens, his reservoir of untapped potentials for development and use in his purpose; and that we are heirs with Jesus Christ and inheritors of the good, perfect, and bountiful gifts. This is Who I Am.

How Shall I Treat My Body?

Central to much of the battle for urban youth is the lesson that one's body is not one's own. It is a gift from God and has been bought at a great price. It is the temple in which the Holy Spirit dwells. The Bible teaches that God is to be glorified in the body (1 Corinthians 6:19). Alcohol, sexual immorality, life-killing drugs, crime, and abuse of children, youth, and adults gravely afflict our society and nation. No one questions that actual threat to the physical health of youth in the city. God wants his human creations to use every part of their bodies to give glory back to him.

What or Whom Should We Worship?

In these days it is especially important to realize that we cannot assume our people, especially our youth, have an adequate understanding of worship. It seems a category strange and unfamiliar to many since they do not realize the attention they give to the role models and ambitions around them is in fact worship. They cannot see the calls to worship that surround them in the neighborhood and on the street and in the media. That we worship God through Jesus Christ, not man-made idols, is a neglected lesson. Man-made idols can neither love, forgive, have compassion and patience, or be merciful. Individuals who make them are like them; so are all who trust in them (Psalm 115:3-8).

God is the anointing Spirit that sustains all things, and they that worship him must do so in spirit and truth. He is all powerful and all-wise. No person, no circumstance, no group, no condition—however alarming or threatening—can frustrate, obstruct, defeat, or negate him; for he is love, good, and his steadfast love and faithful promises endure forever. He has placed eternity in the heart of his creations; they cannot be at peace until they find him. We teach that it is God alone that we worship. We teach it in our words, but most importantly we teach it by the lives we live *with* our students in the regular patterns of urban church life.

What Is God's Church—and What Is It Not?

As church educators, we must remember that God's church is not a place or building, though elaborate in architectural design, modern equipment, and furnishings; not the preacher, though gifted in speech, dynamic in personality, and dramatic in ability to draw multitudes to hear him or her speak and preach; not the choir(s) elaborately robed and assistant to the pastor as "singing ministers" in the worship service; and not the stewards, trustees, deacons, elders, though some individuals, boards, and clubs think so.

The church is not the Sunday school or the CCD with the specific task to teach the word of God and inspire children, youth, and adults to apply truth to their daily living; not the Women's Missionary Society; not the presiding elder or district superintendent (or diocesan) vicar general charged with the supervision of a number of churches; and not the bishops, who carry the office of awesome power, authority, and responsibility practically unlimited.

Certainly, the church is not any other kind of organization other than "the body of Christ in the world to seek and save sinners."

WHAT IS RACISM?

We cannot shrink from identifying social realities in our religious education work. We teach that racism is the belief that race is the primary determinant of human traits and capacities and that racial differences produce an inherent superiority or inferiority of a particular race. No one can honestly deny that racism pervades America and finds some of its most fertile ground in the dynamics of urban America. It is interwoven in every fabric of contemporary American society. It manifests itself in individual attitudes, acts, policies, procedures, decisions, and practices of secular *and* religious institutional structures and organizations.

American Negroes (blacks), Puerto Ricans, Mexicans, Japanese, Chinese, and Native Indians are specifically affected, blacks more because of their "skin color" and historic slavery experience. Methodist bishops in a recent statement pointed to the current status of this condition:

> The malignancy of racism, though more subtle than in previous years, remains an integral part of life. In fields of education, within business, industrial and corporate life, in government and even in religion, people are judged and treated according to the color of their skin rather than competency and the content of their character. As a result, we are seeing problems of economic injustice, lack of educational opportunity, unequal protection under the law, and increasing social dislocations. We call upon the people called Methodist and all others to mobilize moral, spiritual, and legal resources to eradicate the evils of racism.[1]

We teach that Jesus, in his life of love, suffering, and forgiveness, pointed the way to confront racism and the accompanying dehumanizing effects when he said, "Love your enemies, do good to those who hate you. Bless those who curse you, and pray for those who abuse you. . . . And as you wish that men would do to you, do so to them (Luke 6:27, 28, 31).

Martin Luther King Jr., a contemporary prophet, a Nobel laureate, a crusader not only for black people but for all humanity, left as an eternal legacy a philosophy of nonviolent direction as the truest passionate concern that transcends class, sexism, age, creed, and respect for the dignity and worth of every human being, and a "dream" that one day our nation will rise up and live the true meaning of its creed: "All men are created equal." Ordained preacher, teacher, and disciple, he exhorted America to share his dream of a better world.

In sum total, King's legacy is one to end Negro servitude and human enslavement wherever in existence, leaving no doubt in compassionate hearts and alert minds that the destiny of America and all humankind is inextricably *one*. We teach that racism is a reality, but God's power to change is a greater reality.

WHAT IS THE CONTINUING BURDEN OF SLAVERY?

Blacks, uniquely visible, continue to bear the marks of the afflictions, sufferings, and deprivations of their tragic and dehumanizing experience of their slavery. These marks effect the educational challenge of the church.

Ignorance of these marks among teachers and aides in secular and religious institutions, among persons in other settings that deal with educational experiences, continues to be appalling and dangerous. The crime and social sin of that experience has yet to be acknowledged fully and dealt with effectively by families, secular authorities, and the Christ-centered church. The facts must be taught with spiritual understanding. Historical facts as given by Benjamin Elijah Mays and Joseph William Nicholson may be considered as an integral part of the urban church's religious education work!

The tragedy of slavery did not lie in the fact that the slave worked long hours, that he had too little of food and clothing, that he was often flogged, or even that he was sometimes sold away from his family. The tragedy lay in the fact that *from infancy he was so conditioned and trained by precept and the collective expectation of his own inferiority and to accept his servile status as a matter of course. The slave system could continue to exist because it had made of him a slave in mind as well as in body.* This was the crime of slavery, and in part, of the plantation itself, and from the shadow the Negro masses have not yet wholly emerged.[2]

We must not pretend that the burden of the effects of slavery is not even to this day a major factor in the educational as well as social ministry of the church, both black and white.

WHAT IS THE CALL TO THE BLACK CHURCH?

We teach about the future of the black church knowing that critical analysis of the history of the black church in urban religious education activity gives insight to all of those with concern in religious education in an urban setting. The Emancipation Proclamation signed September, 1862, became effective January 1, 1863. But even then the black church was forced to build an exclusive institution that provided for the social life and economic necessities as an alternative society that said "yes" to its people when white society said "no!"

The black church nurtured pride and self-respect within the mass of legally emancipated slaves who otherwise would have been beaten by life and completely submerged. It shared love, gave hope, and showed appreciation. It was so important that the black church and the black preacher be truly Christian, truly prophetic, and truly active with Christ in reconciling work. The black church organized training schools which gave the masses of the race an opportunity to develop mind, body, and soul, and the self-expression that no other enterprise in society offered. It gave to thousands and thousands unable to own homes a sense of pride of ownership. Its slavery-conditioned members contributed music, laughter, dance, drama, and skill in building our nation and in weaving the complex fabric of civilization in the Western world.

The record of history must be taught today, taught by the church, taught to those who might otherwise never know. We must teach how the black church, with its face to the rising sun, developed a genius to struggle for survival as it lived under the most perilous circumstances to achieve freedom. Owned and supported by poor people as their meager incomes allowed, it built a freedom for their pastors to preach the gospel, 1) standing firm with the God of the oppressed, poor, and powerless, 2) preaching the gospel of Jesus Christ, and 3) applying it to economic and political oppressions.

The 200th anniversary of our national Constitution, gloriously celebrated, has passed, leaving behind "freedoms" yet to be achieved. The black church must continue to challenge, to struggle, and to provide leadership—not only to achieve long overdue social, economic, political, and educational freedoms for its own people but for the *liberation* of all humankind to share what the Constitution exclaims and the gospel of Jesus Christ the churches of believing Christians proclaim.

This is the call that reaches the black church and empowers it in its various ministries. It is this call that also empowers the will to teach.

PRINCIPLES OF MOTIVATING POWER

The viable urban church religious education program in "making disciples" must give special attention to motivation. Matters of the will and attention to hope are desperately needed by ethnic minority children, youth, and adults in the arena of urban life today. The power of the inspiration may come from persons of lowly birth, from those known only through their biographies, through those in positions of leadership, even those "unsung persons" who know the Lord. But God's word is the basic source.

My mother is my example of the inspiring teacher. Born of parents of slavery, she had only a seventh-grade education. Despite this, she became an elementary school teacher and a grassroots church and community social worker in Georgia in the rural town "racist" environment where she was born. She knew the Lord and vowed in her heart that her children would have a Christian education as long as she lived. I faithfully share the following ten principles that she taught with the confidence that they are as relevant today as they were those many years ago, and as relevant to the urban church as they were to my own rural beginnings:

1. As God's children, always love God and treat every person as God's child.
2. Take what you have and make what you want, and your skills and abilities will always make room for you.
3. Never allow anyone to drag you so low as to make you hate, for hate destroys, finally, the hater.
4. Burn the midnight oil to achieve your goals, and always study to become an approved workman of God; achieve excellence.
5. Have respect for education and stop not short of the highest possible level you can attain; in your faith and work whatever is for you, you will get.
6. Develop a smiling face and always be gracious to everyone, even though everyone is not gracious to you; and by all means treat others as you want others to treat you.
7. Stay with the church and be a person to work for change to improve the surroundings wherever you find yourself.
8. Your body is a temple of God; do nothing to mar or destroy it.
9. In all that you do, do it to help somebody.
10. Always raise your eyes to the hills from whence help comes. God, who made the hills, the mountains, the earth and heaven, and everything in them, can and will open doors for you that no one else can open and no one can shut.

THE IMPORTANCE OF DEVELOPING
CHRISTIAN LEADERS

Education is the prime factor in leadership development, and leadership is the critical dimension of our current situation and the key to the future. The general function of leadership is "to define purpose, to interpret these purposes into practical goals, to clarify the assignment of responsibilities, to guide the processes of planning, to open up the potential ties of available resources, to keep operations consistent with purposes and goals, to maintain action and change continuously, and to evaluate efforts and results."[3]

The basic process is planning and keeping Christ in the center of all activities, deeds, acts, program resources, movements, and processes to win people to a personal commitment to Jesus as Lord and Savior. In most churches, the pastor, as spiritual leader of the local church, must also be the chief leader of the religious education program.

Qualified teachers in the religious education program should be persons who bear the earmarks of a Christian life, who know biblical truths, and who can communicate these truths to learners. They should be persons who subject their minds and hearts and wills wholly to God. Jesus said, "Not my will, Father, but thine."

THE PLACE FOR THE INCLUSIVE CHURCH

I have written at some length here of the role of the black church. Is there a place for the inclusive church? The "church body" has always been and is now a mixture of diverse people — poor and affluent, illiterate and learned, young and elderly, saved and unsaved, obedient and disobedient, black and non-black, peace-keepers and trouble-makers, honest and dishonest, faithful and nonfaithful. But freedom-of-religion laws allow the "wheat and the weeds" to grow together. The purpose of the church is to increase the love of God and neighbor. The mission is "making disciples" for Jesus. Therefore the ultimate goal is the inclusive church.

An inclusive church is one that must begin with the minds and hearts of believing Christians: people who pray it, say it, sing it, shout it, share it, and BE it to God's glory. Through it can be established a sense of unity among people and nations, as well as a world harboring a vision of love and peace.

Melvin Talbert, a bishop, states that "inclusiveness" means persons bring to society who they are—their whole sense of history—and they need not abandon or deny it in order to be accepted or in order to find wholeness and meaning.

Inclusiveness affirms all persons as creatures of God—minority and majority—who exist. . . in community, which means that all persons make their contributions out of the context of their own history and identity.[4]

Inclusiveness involves justice and liberation and mission. Community outreach by an inclusive urban church living in "togetherness" can provide moral leadership, stability, and unity to eliminate racism in all of its forms in the church and society of America. These creative opportunities are available to Christian leadership in the pursuit and promotion of inclusiveness:

1. Fellowship and unity around the table of the Holy Supper Celebration in accord with the divine standard of equality.
2. A look—candid, honest, courageous—by the church itself by calling acts of injustice and dishonor by their real names and by Bible truth education, examining its own attitudes, emotions, and behavior patterns to *uncover* the subtle and conscious forms of negative racism embedded therein.
3. Issuance of the divine call to recognize its own contribution to racism, to repent, and with God's help to make adjustments and the necessary changes to the glory of God.
4. Making the church building a place of assembly in which ecumenical, educational, social, political, and religious movements can gather in freedom to plan strategies to make neighborhoods, communities, and the world a fit place for human beings to live.

The principle of "inclusiveness" is a challenge to us all to promote a ministry of service to the hungry, the homeless, the unclothed, the imprisoned; and attack the dehumanizing and ungodly illnesses of the soul.

As we move into the twenty-first century, racism and exclusiveness are excess baggage to an "inclusive church," a powerful church, a faithful church. The church, the "body of Christ," is God's instrument of salvation in the world. Therefore, it must acknowledge its social sin of exclusiveness, face issues honestly, and make unlimited sacrifices in all of its ministries, especially education, to achieve meaningful equality of opportunity for all citizens and a true proclamation of the gospel of Jesus Christ.

The urban church in its religious education work of "making disciples" cannot achieve its goal if not anointed by the Holy Spirit. With that anointing, the teaching shall be followed by learning, and learning by faithful discipleship.

NOTES

1. African Methodist Epsicopal Church, African Methodist Episcopal Zion Church, Christian Methodist Episcopal Church, and United Methodist Church in their Fourth Consultation, Washington, D.C. Statement published in *The Christian Index*, Official Organ of the C.M.E. Church, Vol. 120, No. 8, April 15, 1987, p. 9.

2. Benjamin Elijah Mays and Joseph William Nicholson, *The Negro Church* (New York: Negro University Press, 1933), p. 1.

3. Wilbur C. Hollenbeck, Teachers College Columbia University, New York, N.Y. and my doctor of education advisor, 1953-1954.

4. Melvin G. Talbert, "A More Meaningful Witness in Black Communities," *Priority Concern of Black United Methodists*, November 1980, p. 18.

Chapter 10

Doing Your Own
Urban Church Research

Laurence L. Falk

Mt. Auburn Church is located in an urban neighborhood that has undergone almost continuous change for the past thirty years. The neighborhood has a history that reflects days of rather prestigious wealth. It was then passed by as other neighborhoods, newer and different in housing style, became favored. Then it found itself in the midst of racial transition as whites moved out and blacks moved in. Later there was a class change as large houses were turned into multiple family rental units and public housing was built for low income, primarily black families. Still later the area saw an influx of professionals who changed the large houses into offices for their services— mostly medical but also legal and related professionals. Of late some gentrification has begun with the problems related to displacement of the poor by those able to remodel housing for high-income people.

A new pastor was called to the church and began to wonder, along with the people of the church, just what was the situation? What was the composition of the resident neighborhood? What were the needs of those in the neighborhood that a church might address? They had a desire for information and a hunch that they needed to do some research. Their good fortune was that a college professor with capabilities in communi-

114

ty research was available to them as a consultant. They began to learn from him.

A Consultant's Advice

They learned that many persons working in religious organizations need information about their community, but the required information is often lacking. The options are to make decisions based on what is already known or to carry out research that will provide the needed information. Employing professional researchers to do investigating is usually beyond the resources of church organizations because systematic scientific research may cost from several to many thousands of dollars depending on the kind of information needed. Nevertheless church personnel can gather much adequate information within the financial limits of the local church.

Good Research Is Not a Matter of Money Only

The amount of money spent on research does not appreciably alter the routines followed in gathering information. The research process among the sciences is fairly standard. Most research begins with a problem area requiring more information. The researcher gathers literature pertaining to the problem and develops a research method for gathering the specific information needed. The research is implemented, findings analyzed, and conclusions drawn. These conclusions provide the basis for making decisions about the original problem. What varies among research projects is thoroughness, depth of statistical analysis, and perhaps mode of reporting. Understanding the basic routines of information gathering will help local church personnel do their own community research.

Asking the Right Questions

Mt. Auburn church learned what seemed to be obvious but could have been easily neglected, that is, community research requires asking the right questions of appropriate persons or information sources. First, one must clarify the dimensions of the problem requiring more information. The interested people of Mt. Auburn Church gathered together to think through this first step. What did they really want to know? They thought that some general numerical data would be of interest. How many of these and how many of those? But they began to realize that numbers alone would not give them the direction they wanted in developing a more relevant ministry to that neighborhood. They knew they could be misled by the data if they only asked some very general questions. It is possible that what might appear to be a need on the basis of the numbers would not be real need as the people of the neighborhood saw the situation. The researchers must be clear about the specific problem needing answers.

Getting Help from Others

The task looked large even when modestly stated. Then they learned it is not always necessary to gather one's own information. General information is usually available about most communities, though it is often the case that information is not quite in the form needed, that it is too old, or that it would take more time to acquire than gathering one's own information. Nevertheless, it is better to check for existing information before gathering one's own.

Two Kinds of Research—Two Kinds of Data

Researchers usually distinguish between two kinds of information, qualitative and quantitative. Qualitative information uses descriptive narrative based on information provided from personal interviews and detailed observations of persons and events. Qualitative information is more difficult to analyze than quantitative because it is more experiential and definitional. But it has the advantage of including nuances of feelings, attitudes, and opinions not represented in numbers. Since getting detailed information is time-consuming, the number of cases in this kind of study is often limited. For this reason, one may not always know to what degree the information truly represents the study group or event.

Quantitative information is numerical and permits statistical analysis. Questionnaires yielding this kind of information have fixed responses that can be arrayed in tables showing averages, percentages, and so forth. Groups are easier to compare when numbers represent their characteristics. For instance, one might compare the number of single-parent family persons to those with two parents in the family in reference to the need for a day care program. It is not always necessary, in interpreting quantitative reports, that users know the esoteric language of statistical analysis to understand their implications. The tables in published reports are usually summarized in forthright language. After all, the importance of numbers is in their implications, not in the numbers as such. In sum, the general difference between quantitative and qualitative information is in having more representation through larger numbers of cases (quantitative) or more depth of understanding from fewer cases (qualitative). In either case, the author's interpretation of the study is what one is after.

The Mt. Auburn group knew that they wanted both kinds of information. They wanted some numbers, but they also wanted some carefully researched opinions. The former was a quantitative research process. The latter would be qualitative.

Who Has Already Done Some Research?

They were told that the first step in locating existing information is in the local library. Libraries in cities and those associated with colleges or universities are more likely to contain desired information. However, smaller libraries may have information of local relevance that larger ones would not bother with. The Bureau of the Census publishes much quantitative information. The two basic publications for each state are "General Social and Economic Characteristics" and "Detailed Characteristics." In these, persons are subdivided by county and city or town into characteristics such as age, gender, kind of household, marital status, employment status, kind of occupation, income, parent tongue, ethnic identity, and so on. Some data is available by census tract. Librarians may know if the community did a special census since the last general national census done every ten years.

City and county governments frequently carry out special studies for a variety of reasons. If the community is large enough to have a professional planner, the planning office will be a good source of information. Most of this information is available to the public even though it may not have been well-publicized.

Other Resources of Available Data

So far, mostly governmental sources have been discussed. In deciding to look for information, first decide which community institution is likely to have the desired information. To this end, begin by identifying the major institutional categories in the community. In addition to the governmental, there are the legal, judicial, legislative, educative, economic, welfare, family, recreational, and of course, the religious.

Some of the agencies that were already present in the neighborhood of the Mt. Auburn Church were known to the interest group. They included a neighborhood council, a neighborhood recreation committee, and a senior citizens center. Some inquiry turned up the fact that there was a business-oriented planning group coming into existence. The telephone directory was of help in determining which community organizations were likely to have relevant information.

Also, it is possible that other groups already have information that is pertinent. In the personal computer age, some groups have become rather sophisticated in data acquisition and storage. Should this be true, and the group is willing to share such information, this would save considerable time and expense. If not, it may be possible to carry out cooperative research with other groups that share similar interests. The Mt. Auburn group discovered that a rather dated religious interest survey report was available from a prior cooperative church research effort.

Sources of Qualitative Data

Guidelines for locating qualitative information are similar to that of quantitative, though there may be more sources available. Local newspapers are usually a good source of information. They indicate what kinds of organizations are active in the community, when they meet, their officers, and their interests. Lists gleaned from the newspaper can provide contact points for the research. Of course, organizations may not always wish to share their information. In any case, the organization may be willing to suggest alternative sources. Particularly important would be groups providing human services such as counseling, care for the aged, the indigent, and so on.

The Mt. Auburn people found that a report from the City Planning Commission focused on some very useful "quality of life" issues. Of great significance was that the report had just recently been updated on a mid-way census basis. They also discovered that some interesting historical information was available in the file on their neighborhood from a City Historical Society. Community histories may be available in various forms discussing such things as kinship networks, early experiences, disaster events, ethnic populations, and economic shifts.

The Mt. Auburn research process began with the gathering together of the available reports. That took some time, and reading them was not that easy. They had to learn how to make sense of tables and sort out the portions of the reports that were focused on their geographic area of interest. The general picture they found was that the quality of life, measured in terms of income and housing and jobs and need for government assistance had actually deteriorated in the past five years. The neighborhood *looked* much better since much of that large housing was being restored. But the looks were deceiving.

What Resources Are Available To Do a Survey?

They then realized that they needed more data and would have to do some research on their own. The next option was to determine how to gather it, and this meant doing a survey. Before beginning a survey, they were advised that it is good to take stock of available resources such as time and persons available for developing questionnaires, phoning, stuffing envelopes, and compiling responses. In addition, there is the cost of paper, envelopes, and stamps although the cost of materials is usually relatively small compared to time and effort needed in doing a survey. Before beginning, determine if computer services are available. Personal computers can be used for a variety of tasks including writing reports and counting the responses. Many businesses and homes use small computers, and it is worth determining if these might be used by knowledgeable, and perhaps volunteer, persons. Even though it is not likely that highly sophisticated statistical analysis is desired, the computer is very helpful in counting responses by category and calculating statistics. Of course, this can also be done by hand and percentages figured with pocket calculators.

Sufficient human and financial resources were determined to be available and a survey was found to be necessary. The next task was to formulate a series of questions that would address the primary informational problem. They had already found that a small task force of persons skilled in writing, knowledge-able about the research subject, and interested in the commu-nity is valuable in doing this. Even if a task force had not been used, they would have been better off to have knowledgeable persons examine the questions before duplicating the final questionnaire. Also, they were helped to see that they should administer a preliminary form of the questionnaire to persons similar to the survey respondents. This is well worth the time, as it tends to eliminate unclear questions and problems with questionnaire format. Also it helps to eliminate language that is offensive to or not easily understood by potential respondents. Only after such pretesting is it wise to complete the survey.

Preparing the Questionnaire

They then had to think through the survey process itself. Each survey method has its advantages and disadvantages whether done by mail, telephone, or personal interview. Ques-tionnaires administered by telephone are usually shorter than mailed ones, but the questions may be more open-ended. It is possible to probe more deeply during phone conversations. Of course, open-ended questions in mailed surveys are fine, but the respondent is not able to ask for clarification of questions. Whether phoning, mailing, or doing a personal interview, fixed responses are easier to analyze than are open-ended ones. However, the more open-ended the question, the more likely it is to allow for unanticipated responses. It is up to the surveyor to decide whether ease of analysis or being thorough is to take priority.

The form of the mailed questionnaire is more important than the form of the one used in phoning or personal interviews because the questioner is not present to clarify and explain. In any case, the flow of questions ought to follow a logical se-quence. If personal questions are included, these are better left toward the end of the questionnaire. Questions about money are usually the most sensitive. If you need this information, use categories such as "Under $9,999," "10,000 to 14,999," "14,000 to 19,999," etc., rather than asking for a specific annual income. Most surveys use household rather than personal income.

An important consideration in asking questions is determining the kind of desired response. A "yes," "no," or "no opinion" fixed response may be sufficient. In other cases a scale may be provided. An example would be, "decidedly yes," "yes," slightly yes," "neither yes or no," "slightly no," "no," and "decidedly no." Values may be assigned to these for analysis such as "decidedly yes = 7," "yes = 6," etc. Another way of obtaining responses to fixed categories is to list options and have respondents indicate their preference by ranking the items assigning "1" to the most preferred, "2" to the next preferred, and so on. Of course, one can simply ask the question and permit respondents to answer as they wish. As discussed above, this makes analysis much more difficult. Common sense is usually a good guide to questionnaire construction in that it be neat, uncrowded, readable, and readily understood.

Some introduction to the survey is necessary in all survey methods. Inform the potential respondent about the general purpose of the survey, who is doing it, and why it is important to answer the survey questions. It may be appropriate to give the community advance notice of a survey through the local papers or radio stations if it is going to reach quite a few people. Persons doing the personal or phone survey might practice their routine with a person they know who might help them develop their conversational style. Again, common sense about politeness, patience, and not becoming upset by turndowns or insults will go a long way.

The interest group, now a task force of the church, began the process of thinking through just what they wanted to ask and how they wanted to ask it. They knew that they wanted more number data and some in-depth interviews. What else they needed was not yet clear. Who should they ask?

Who Should You Ask?
Their consultant agreed that perhaps the most difficult part of surveying is deciding whom to survey. If specific information

is needed from all persons in a particular segment of the community, such as what religious affiliation they have, then it is necessary to attempt to contact all these persons. However, if you wish to determine how the community feels about a particular social or religious issue, then a sample of the community is appropriate. There are piles of literature discussing appropriate sampling methods, and the professional researchers argue a good deal about this. Decisions about local churches usually do not require such exact sampling. One thing to keep in mind is that getting responses from larger numbers of persons may produce no more accuracy in representation than smaller ones. The task is to determine who is representative and seek their responses. It is better to ask your questions of only 5 or 10 percent of the target population if it is representative than to ask 50 percent if it is not representative. Use a sample that best represents the population.

There are various ways of selecting a sample. If you know your community fairly well then you can select which group in the community will be most relevant and sample only those areas. For example, suppose one selects twelve city blocks that represent a cross section of the population by age, ethnic identity, gender, and income. Persons are interviewed in every second, third, or fourth household in these blocks depending on the size sample desired. Some samples are obtained from phone directories by selecting every Nth household (eighth, tenth, or twelfth entry, again depending on size of sample desired). The selection should begin by randomly selecting a number between one and ten if it is to be a 10 percent sample and then selecting every tenth household through the directory.

The Telephone Sample

Obtaining a telephone sample is not quite as easy as it appears since not all households have phones, some numbers are not listed, or a household has more than one phone number listed. Also, most surveys separate residence and business telephones. The basic purpose of random sampling is to provide an equal chance for selecting any one unit from the population being studied. Put another way, all names of persons are to be in the hat before the blindfolded person begins drawing the names out. The sampling task is to get all the names in the hat, or at least a cross sectional representation of them, and then randomly draw out some predetermined proportion of the names, such as eight, ten, or twelve percent.

Some surveys may not require a random sample. For instance, perhaps one wishes to obtain a list of community social services and the agencies providing these services. In some communities this information is available. If it is necessary to compile a list, the phone book will provide a starting point. Agencies may have brochures and other available information about their services. The next task is to organize the information into some coherent whole. Since agency services overlap, the study may also need to examine the communicational network among the agencies. Follow-up contacts may be necessary to establish this network.

Contrary to popular wisdom, numbers do not speak for themselves. Interpreting and presenting information requires as much sensitivity and understanding as does gathering it. There are two main questions to be answered in presenting information. How can it best be organized and presented so as to answer the original research question? How can it best be organized and presented for persons to understood and use the information? One will take a different approach if the information is to be presented orally than if it is to be in written form.

Research in Process

The Mt. Auburn Church research process went forward. They did some research by mail of random addresses just to see if the data there was comparable to what they had from the existing reports. They did some selective interviewing of people who seemed to know quite a bit about the neighborhood from their long residency and involvement. They also discovered that they could do some research just by listening carefully to the conversations that went on in the four groups already at work in the neighborhood. That is, they did research by attending meetings and talking to the people there about the interests the church had.

They began to see a much clearer picture of what needs were present, which were already being addressed by other groups, and where the holes were. They couldn't do everything that needed to be done, but they did come up with some conclusions and recommendations. Their task then was to sift the data in order to prepare the reports.

Preparing Reports
They saw that for general audiences and readers it is good to organize quantitative data into straightforward tables. As stated earlier, it is possible to do complex statistical analyses, but for much decision making converting numbers into percentages is adequate. If persons are available who are able to put information on computers, programs are available that digest and organize information into presentable form. It is not imperative that these be available; volunteers are very useful in accomplishing the analysis and report writing. Also, recheck information and data in order to minimize embarrassing errors.

Preparing for an Oral Report
If the presentation is oral, it is best to transfer the pertinent information onto turnover charts or duplicate the information. An example of data presentation is as follows:

Table 1: PERSONS FAVORING BUILDING A NEW CHURCH BY FREQUENCY OF ATTENDANCE

	Regular Church Attenders		Infrequent Church Attenders		None Church Attenders		No Response		Total	
	#	%	#	%	#	%	#	%	#	%
Favoring building a new church in the community	123	47.5	88	34.0	36	13.9	12	4.6	259	100.0

Source: Survey completed by St. Johns

Interpreting the Research
Interpretive skills are important in understanding qualitative information. A first step might be to go through the recorded responses (to open-ended questions) and underline key words

in much the same way one carefully reads a book for content. Then the key words and ideas might be lifted out and organized into categories. One may or may not wish to record the number of times a work or idea appears. If a response occurs only once, it usually does not have the same importance as one that occurs often. However, if one is seeking new options and ideas, the unique response may be important. Interpretation of responses depends on how they relate to the original question or research problem.

The principles used to formulate the survey questionnaire are also used in writing the report, whether it is based on qualitative or quantitative information. Questions to be answered by the report include: Who are the persons reading and interpreting the report? How will the report be used to make decisions? What language is most appropriate for the audience? What standards are there for writing and reporting? At this point, care in questionnaire formulation and respondent selection pays off since information is only as good as the questions asked and the integrity of the respondents in answering them.

Making a Decision

The reports were prepared for the congregation and for other groups that the church thought needed to be brought to an awareness of some unmet needs. They knew that their best ministry might be to mobilize other groups instead of trying to do everything with their limited human and financial resources. They found their own focus of direct urban religious education in the development of a day care program for the young children of single parents who needed short-term help as they got started in a job, finished some schooling, went job hunting, and/or made more permanent arrangements.

The consultant said, "Now don't forget to thank all who helped in the research process, the respondents, and the research volunteers. It is quite likely to be the only reward that volunteers receive."

Keep the Reports

The Mt. Auburn group heard one last suggestion. Keep several copies of the final report and questionnaire for future refer-

Chapter 11

Models for Urban Youth Ministry: Goals, Styles, and Contexts

William R. Myers

While many theoretical models have been described in recent youth ministry literature, most urban parishes unfortunately continue to gauge the effectiveness of their youth ministries by the absence or presence of charismatic youth leaders and big youth groups. In another article, critical of this model, I characterized its figurative form as that of a "pyramid" in which the youth worker (paid or volunteer, lay or professional) resides at the top while a few faithful adults gather round, arranging themselves upon the ever descending levels of the pyramid.[1] In such a model, the youth leader plays the role of a "Lone Ranger." The youth group's "power rests with the one who has the silver bullets, and program participants are ministered to. They have no silver bullets of their own."[2] In this model, youth are the recipients of whatever agenda is important to the youth leader.

Four dangers can be seen in such a model of youth ministry. First, youth deeply concerned about personal identity issues often gravitate toward and dangerously sacralize such powerful charismatic leaders. Second, this model mirrors the dominant culture while effectively transmitting its values (hierarchial, individualistic, white, competitive, imperialistic, and usually male). Third, this model usually understands ministry as program, concentrating upon equipping its charismatic leader with an impressive "Bag of Tricks" instead of any depth or system of ministry. Finally, and perhaps most significantly, this model's leaders never last. National averages suggest that any leader who stays with this model in a local congregation for more than two years is a rarity.

Urban churches would do well to reject models of youth ministry like the pyramid in favor of building more holistic models out of the unique influence of: 1) *congregational goals*; 2) *styles*; and, 3) *contexts.* This chapter explores parish adaptations from the pivotal perspectives of these three factors. The strengths and weaknesses of the resulting parish models of religious education for youth are critiqued with the hoped for result of more intentionality on the part of those religious educators and congregations seriously concerned about ministry in the church.

Goals

When we consider the three factors (goal, context, and style), it is the *goal* which initially determines the design of a church's youth ministry model. A "goal" means a pragmatic, attainable, and hoped for outcome to be reached from the use of particular strategies.

For example, Bethel Place, an urban parish, states its youth ministry goal as "protecting our youth while teaching them our faith."[3] Building toward such a double-edged goal, Bethel Place starts its fall program with a new youth choir for its member's children, anchored inside an adult-directed, every-Tuesday-after-school "Bible study and fellowship" group. The choir is to sing twice each month in the Sunday adult worship service.

The form of such a model might figuratively be described as that of a "closed circle." In this model, grown from precise goals, "we" protect "our" youth while faithfully transmitting "our" faith. Such a youth ministry model intentionally separates itself from the surrounding culture. While some ministries might reject both the model and its values, the form follows the logic of Bethel Place's two stated goals. Bethel Place might be challenged by those seeking a more holistic model of youth ministry to reconsider its goals and open its "closed circle" model.[4]

A very different congregation, Lynwood Church, has goals which emerge from that church's activist base: "Youth ministry is to impact, in a positive way, those younger gang members in our neighborhood." In Lynwood's effort "to offer an alternative," the congregation mounts an ambitious package—an after-school and every Saturday Basketball League complete with uniforms, teams, and prizes. Consciously employing positive peer pressure by using older youth and younger adults as leaders, Lynwood names and commissions those persons as their "Basketball Ministry Staff."[5]

Such a model turns the closed circle inside out. It has, however, the possibility of becoming so identified with basketball that it more closely resembles a park district program instead of the religious education work of a church. Perhaps, for Lynwood Church, this is not a problem. Other parishes might demand more visible and deeper connections with the church. I know one urban church with such a program that equates whether or not a team member gets to play in that week's competition on the basis of church attendance. Again, the question of a church's *goals* emerges.[6]

Goals, the "ends" a church hopes to attain, as these churches illustrate, carry within them certain logical consequences. Bethel Place's goals are exclusive: In figurative form they demand a "closed circle." An "open circle" (like Lynwood Church's) does not "fit" the goals of Bethel Place; in similar fashion, the "closed circle" (like Bethel Place's) does not fit Lynwood Church's goals. A clear goal statement is a necessary first step toward determining the appropriate youth ministry model for a particular church. Goals emerge, in part, when a church recognizes that it has a particular "style."

Style

"Style," usually the result of a long-standing sequence of events, can readily be understood by a church as "that's the way we do it." The "we" of this statement usually contains an ethnic/racial/cultural category, as in "we who are black," or "white," or "Hispanics who are Puerto Rican," preach, pray, and sing, in a particular *way*.

The *way* we preach, pray, and sing is respected by us. For example, blacks tend to affirm an expressively emotive and dialogical style of worship while whites tend to be comfortable with worship that is more controlled and monological.[7] In building models of youth ministry, the awareness of the implications of such "styles" provides a congregation with a set of specific reference points.[8]

For example, Grace Church, a large parish on describing themselves as "unashamedly black and unapologetically Christian," struggled early in its existence with questions of style. Some members of the church, affirming a black dialogical style of worship against what they called an "inappropriate pursuit of white middle-classness," sought a more consciously "black style" emotive worship celebration for Grace. Grace's pastor, conscious of this underlying conflict, notes how at that time the congregation decided "to become a black church" within the black community. "Some members left when the first 'Amen' happened in worship," continues the Senior Pastor, "but God blessed us. Today we are that unashamedly black church within the black community."[9]

Qualitative research on black and white middle-class models of religious education for youth indicates that blacks who are critical of their surrounding culture are much more aware of the implications of "style" than are blacks or whites who are unreflective about their positions within that dominant culture.[10]

White "styles" of youth ministry often unreflectively strive to transmit a culture that, by and large, has blessed its members.[11] A consciously "black style" model of youth religious education critically distances itself from a culture which has proven, again and again, to be untrustworthy.[12]

While it follows that a model built with "white style" normally cannot be transplanted into a consciously black youth context, there are black congregations which attempt to use white style models of youth ministry. Critics of such congregations claim those who adopt white style models of youth ministry are tacitly accommodating the white culture's dominant value system. In any case, a white style model is not value neutral. Unless it is radically redirected, it carries values antagonistic to the implications of black style.

Context

As style impacts a church's goals, so context provides a way of summing up the congregation's total present picture. Someone aware of contextual issues has a more holistic understanding of how these three factors (style, goal, context) come together. Things like size, socioeconomic class, and the age of a congregation contextually frame the present possibilities and problems of the congregation. In addition, contextual issues like whether or not laity live within walking distance of the church building and how leadership is concentrated in an authoritative minister and not shared with the laity, including youth, also affect how a particular parish functions. Finally, the ways parish leaders, clergy, and professional religious educators understand their respective (unified or adversarial) theological position(s) regarding ministry contextually qualify certain possibilities for youth religious education.

For example, the context of a white, upper-class, mainline, professionally led, middle-sized, evangelical and more conservative Protestant congregation (where most of the members live outside the neighborhood and are richly "blessed" by the dominant culture) presents a context which, without critical reflection, argues for the addition of more professional religious educators as the "answer" to questions of "who should do" youth ministry. Within such a context, while the choice of another professional religious educator "to do" youth ministry is not inevitable, in such situations a move like this is strongly informed by the overall context of a particular urban parish.

Consider another example, St. John's, a Puerto Rican, mixed-class, mainline Protestant, small, activist congregation with a woman pastor. Most of its members live within walking distance of the church building and are suspicious of the dominant culture. St. John's context, informed by the goal of "equipping our youth with a strong and active faith in order that they might thrive (educationally, vocationally, politically, spiritually) within this often hostile culture," taps certain strengths from its *context* in order to build a more "web-like" model of youth ministry.[13]

St. John's model has five components:

- Cross-generational *family* events: A Puerto Rican congregation with a strong female pastor builds such events from its small-church consciousness around the intimate, extended family Sunday worship.

- Cross-generational *Bible study*: Regularized occasions for involvement in cross-generational Bible study groups assume youth are brother/sister pilgrims in the faith journey. Youth read scripture and present testimony in Sunday worship.

- Critically reflective *Christian Youth Group*: Working with a "team" concept, the pastor and a number of involved adults actively reflect upon the role of the Christian within an essentially hostile culture. Youth are encouraged, out of such reflection, to occasionally preach in the Sunday worship.[14]

- Cross-generational *activist* emphasis: St. John's mainline (moderate to liberal) denomination emphasizes pluralism and the raising of social consciousness. Involved in the political process of its city, St. John "speaks from the pulpit" about politics and regularly involves its youth in this process.[15]

- *Worship*: The Sunday experience radically affirms these four factors. As a result, worship feels like an extended, cross-generational, politically aware, biblically informed, intimate Hispanic family. The metaphoric language of the active Christian is present; youth and adults readily reflect on contemporary issues.

St. John's *goal* for youth ministry, joined to its particular *context* and *style*, becomes (out of many possibilities) a clear model for youth religious education. This model operates in the form of a "congregational web" in which youth are "immersed." Here every adult, by being an active member of this congregation, becomes a "youth minister." Youth immersed in such a model are blessed with rich "faith-shaping" experiences and memories.[16]

Summary

Style (from the past), *context* (in the present) and *goal* (toward the future) come together (explicitly or implicitly) in the building of a certain model for the religious education of urban youth. When a set of normative assumptions about style, context, and particular goals hangs together in a coherent form which can be implemented, supported, and tested that constellation can be said to be a "model." Such models are figurative in that they contain metaphoric instead of literal representations. Congregations adopting the "pyramid," "open circle," "closed circle," and "web" (out of their unique styles, contexts, and goals) adopt the values implicit to each model. Blind or uncritical adoption of certain models because they look good, work pragmatically, or come highly recommended misses the depth issue of what such hidden assumptions imply for the churches accepting them. The best urban youth ministry programs grow naturally out of and reflect the style, context, and goals of their individual urban churches.

Notes

1. William R. Myers, "Church in the World: Models of Youth Ministry," *Theology Today* 44: 1 (April 1987), pp. 103-110.
2. Ibid., p. 104.
3. While the congregational youth models discussed within this article are real, all names have been disguised.
4. Consider, for example, Maria Harris, *Portrait of Youth Ministry* (New York: Paulist, 1981).
5. See Brian Reynolds, *A Chance To Serve: A Leader's Manual For Peer Ministry* (Winona, Minn.: Saint Mary's Press, 1984).
6. See Michael Warren, *Youth, Gospel, Liberation* (New York: Harper & Row, 1987).
7. Thomas Kochman, *Black and White Styles in Conflict* (Chicago: University of Chicago Press, 1981).

8. See Ella P. Mitchell, "Oral Tradition: Legacy of Faith for the Black Church," *Religious Education* 81: 1 (Winter 1986), pp. 93-112.

9. William R. Myers "Grace Church, An Ethnographic Description of a Black Youth Ministry Model," a paper given at *The Association of Professors and Researchers in Religious Education* (A.P.R.R.E.), Chicago, 1985.

10. William R. Myers, "Educational Models for Youth: Black and White Contextual Agendas," a paper presented at *The Society for Research in Child Development* (S.R.C.D.), Baltimore, 1987.

11. Ibid.

12. Ibid.

13. Consider a "web-like" model: Stephen S. Jones, *Faith Shaping: Nurturing the Faith Journey of Youth* (Valley Forge, Pa.: Judson, 1980).

14. Ginny Ward Holderness, *Youth Ministry: The New Team Ministry* (Atlanta: John Knox, 1981).

15. See both Harris, *Portrait* and Warren, *Youth, Gospel, Liberation.*

16. See Jones, *Faith Shaping.*

Chapter 12

Urban Church Growth Through Adult Religious Education

Bill Gambrell

Sunday school was not always for adults! During the first 110 years of its history, this organization limited itself to the instruction of children and youth. But at First Baptist Church, Jackson, Mississippi, Christian education and ministry to adults are carried out through the Sunday school. Adult Sunday school is a priority!

In 1975, the church had one Sunday school session (9:40-10:20 A.M.), which included 30 departments of 3-6 classes each and 180 Sunday school officers and teachers. Under the direction of David Roddy, minister of education, the Sunday school began to emphasize the creation of new units and the enlargement of the organizational structure. By the end of the next year, a second Sunday school session (11:00 A.M. - 12:00 noon) had been started, and the number of departments had grown to a total of 44, with a total of 210 teachers and officers. In an organization regularly creating new units, growth potential is multiplied enormously. In 1980, a third Sunday school session (8:20-9:30 A.M.) was added, and, at this writing, under the direction of Bill Gambrell, minister of education, the Sunday school has grown to 98 departments and has 484 officers and teachers. Twenty-nine departments and 87 classes are geared toward reaching, teaching, and ministering to adults.

Why has First Baptist been able to buck the trend of the last decade toward declining attendance in Sunday school? The answer is that the church has adhered to six basic principles for reaching and teaching adults.

Commitment to Adults

First, the First Baptist Church has made a commitment to reach adults. We believe the church should reach adults, can reach adults, and will reach adults. We believe that every adult in Jackson not involved in some weekly Bible study is a prospect for ours. We are committed to meeting their spiritual needs. Challenging annual enrollment goals are set and monitored. Attendance graphs for each department are reviewed monthly. However, we never look at numbers for numbers' sake. We want each adult who attends Bible study, even once, to go home with certain favorable impressions:
1. That he was welcome and his attendance appreciated;
2. That he met people who will be his friends if he continues;
3. That he was believed if he said that he wanted to be a member of the class. We attempt to enroll every adult on his first visit.
4. That if he continues to attend, he will understand the Bible better and will come to know the Lord Jesus Christ, if he doesn't already.

Training Teachers

Second, we enlist and train teachers and class leaders who care about adults. There are three requirements for adult leaders at First Baptist: they must be born-again believers; they must be members of this local church; and they must love the adults with whom they will be working. We firmly believe that unless the teacher loves the age group with which he will be involved, his religious education work will be ineffective. That does not mean that we are unconcerned about the use of proper teaching methods or the teacher's knowledge of the Bible. Each September we sponsor an Annual Leadership Thank You Banquet. The purpose is threefold: 1) to say "thank you" to those who have served in the past year, 2) to say "thank you" in advance to those who are preparing to serve, and 3) to present

the theme and goals for the new Sunday school year. We also conduct "nuts and bolts" conferences later in the month to prepare leaders for their area of service. The agenda for these conferences includes:
1. Distribution of curriculum materials,
2. Setting of goals,
3. Discussion of responsibility,
4. Distribution of class rosters,
5. Inventory of equipment needs,
6. Update of policies and procedures,
7. Setting of calendar dates,
8. Making room assignments, and
9. Announcing opportunities for training.
In addition, seminars and training conferences that deal with philosophy of education and teaching methods are offered quarterly.

Departments and Classes

Third, we organize our adults into departments and classes for outreach and ministry. The adult class is our primary teaching unit. The majority of our classes are composed of fewer than 35 persons. We have found that when the enrollment reaches many more than 35 the motivation to reach more persons is lessened, and the ability to involve adults in the teaching/learning process is greatly hampered. Small classes allow a teacher to use a variety of methods and visual materials. Room arrangement, as well as class size, can either encourage or discourage participation. When adults are seated around a table or in a circle or U-shape, more discussion is encouraged because they can see each other. When adults are seated more formally in rows, they tend merely to listen to the teacher and answer his questions. Each adult class has, in addition to the teacher, an outreach leader, several group leaders, and an activities leader. The outreach leader is responsible for cultivating prospects for the class. Group leaders are responsible for personal ministry to 4-6 persons in the class through regular contact by telephone or home visits, get-well and birthday cards, and additional personal attention that emphasizes the importance of each individual. The activities leader works with the

class outreach leader in week-time activities and has major responsibility for ministry to class members. We have found that
the building of fellowship in adult classes is an important aspect
of the education process. There is a common myth today that
says that adults attend Sunday school classes primarily to learn.
Our adults come to study the Bible, but they also come to meet
friends. We provide coffee and Cokes in many adult departments to promote fellowship and informal periods of sharing.
We feel that some important learning takes place through informal conversation with respected peers during the time before
and after the lesson. Class projects are also instrumental in
strengthening classes and involving members in ministry. Although we believe in and promote unified budget giving, many
of our classes have adopted class ministry projects such as
tutoring disadvantaged children, remodeling the Baptist Mission Center, providing toys, food, and clothing for needy children at Christmas, and supporting individual missionaries. Every adult learner wants his or her life to count for something,
and we have seen adults regain their sense of worth as they
worked with other class members on such projects. We feel
enlisting these additional class officers makes for a more effective ministry, allows the teacher to spend more time in weekly
lesson preparation, involves a greater number of adults, provides a training ground for new leadership, permits more persons to share in the blessings of Christian service, and increases
attendance.

New Classes

Fourth, we start new adult classes annually. Each spring we
examine the adult division of our Sunday school, looking at
existing classes and analyzing potential areas of growth. New
classes are created based on the number of prospects in particular age groups. We have found that new adult units often:
1. Grow more rapidly,
2. Resolve personality conflicts,
3. Minister more effectively,
4. Foster Christian growth and enthusiasm,
5. Provide progressive Bible study experiences that meet
   members' needs,

6. Produce an enlarged Sunday school attendance. (Adults bring preschoolers and children, while the revesre is not always true.)

Classes are also started to reach similar kinds of people. Several years ago it was discovered that a number of young couples in the church were going to be married around the same time. A class was begun for newly marrieds. Today that class has 74 members and has "birthed" 3 additional classes of 40 persons each in the past 5 years. In the mid-1970s, a class was started for single adults. Today First Baptist ministers to over 1,100 single adults in 7 departments and 24 classes.

Space and Equipment

Fifth, we provide space and equipment for adult classes. A famous East Texas philosopher once said, "You can only put so many marshmallows in a Coke bottle." Believe it or not, that statement has had meaning for our adult classes and departments. We have found that once attendance reaches 80-85 percent capacity of the room the potential for growth ceases. Each year we seek to provide adequate adult education space by:

1. Analyzing the space available. Sketches of floor plans have been produced with the square footage of each room recorded.
2. Determining the amount of space needed. By looking at the projected number of classes needed, we compute the number and size of classrooms needed. We attempt to provide 10-12 square feet of space for each adult we want to reach.
3. Reassigning space. Due to the growth or lack of growth of certain classes, space is reassigned.
4. Multiplying the use of space. Some adult classrooms are used by as many as 4 classes on a given Sunday.
5. Securing additional space. Currently, we have classes meeting on 5 different city blocks.
6. Constructing new space. In 6 months, we will move into approximately 25,000 square feet of new adult education facilities.

Not only is adequate space needed, but so is adequate equipment. Each adult classroom is equipped with chalkboards, bulletin boards, and storage cabinets. Teachers have access to overhead projectors, cassette players, filmstrip projectors, and video recorders. We also attempt to provide adult space that has adequate ventilation, non-glare lighting, comfortable seats, and appealing wall and floor coverings.

Teaching the Bible

Sixth, we teach the Bible to win the lost and develop the saved. It is a well-known fact that many adults who have long attended Bible-believing churches know little of the Bible. We have other programs designed to teach nonbiblical subjects; our Sunday school hour is primarily for Bible study. Our curriculum, which is predominantly uniform throughout the adult division, provides for a study of specific books of the Bible and covers the entire Bible in nine years. The overarching objective of this curriculum is to help persons become aware of God as revealed in Jesus Christ, respond to God in a personal commitment of faith, strive to follow God in the full meaning of Christian discipleship, live in a conscious recognition of the guidance and power of the Holy Spirit, and grow toward the goal of Christian maturity. We strive for teaching that is:

1. Incarnational—This simply means that "the word is made flesh" in the life of the teacher and in the lives of adult class members. We expect our teachers to be a cut above, in terms of their ethical and moral values. We seek teachers who are "living the scriptures."
2. Informed—It is an old, threadbare adage, to be sure, but it still is true that the best teachers "teach out of the overflow." They know more than they say. We attempt to prepare our teachers to speak out of a broad repertoire of knowledge gained through diligent preparation and to be flexible and open to teachable moments.
3. Person-centered—We encourage each adult teacher to visit in the home of each class member at least twice a year. Only through these encounters do teachers learn of private frustration anxieties and aspirations of members. Bob Barnett accepted the assignment of teaching a young men's Sunday school class. The class had five men enrolled, but only one of those men ever attended. Bob invited each of the other

four men to lunch. He also contacted each husband of the members of the ladies' class, and invited him to lunch. Not only has his class grown to an average attendance of 21 men per Sunday, but he is able to teach more effectively because of the bridges he has built with these men.

4. Spirit-led—Each of our adult teachers is encouraged to clothe in prayer their efforts in personal study of the scriptures, in lesson preparation, and in classroom activities. No teacher can guarantee that desired learnings will happen, but every teacher can set the stage for the renewing of minds and the transformation of lives through the work of the Spirit.

Operating Principles

We also attempt to observe the following principles in each of our adult classes:

1. No Christian has a monopoly on understanding either God's Word or the words of the scripture. This includes biblical scholars and the most unlearned class member. Each of us must listen to one another as we seek to understand the richness of God's gifts.
2. Few of us will know Hebrew or Greek, and we, therefore, need to use a variety of English versions to try to understand the text itself.
3. While we accept differences among us, we do not feel that those differences are unimportant, nor that they should be ignored or treated as if they did not matter.
4. Different biblical understandings can remain between us, and we can still be warm, Christian friends. In fact, as we grow to better understand our differences, we can grow in our appreciation of one another.

At First Baptist Church, we believe that spiritual changes in the life of the adult learner are dependent on the study of God's Word. Sunday school classes can reach more adults and teach more Bible than any other organization. Adult Sunday school is a top priority.

Chapter 13

Biblical Storytelling in the City

Tom Boomershine

A Personal Story

Thinking about the potential role of biblical storytelling in urban religious education makes me think of our wedding day, twenty-four years ago, and Joe. As my wife, Jean, and I look over our wedding pictures each year, there in the midst of a group of older white folks who gathered at New York's Union Theological Seminary's chapel is one teenager, a striking, six-teen-year-old black young man. Joe was from Brooklyn and was part of the youth program at Duryea Presbyterian Church on the edge of Bedford-Stuyvesant, where I was working part time. Joe was the only person from Duryea who came to the wedding and the only black. You who know the realities of urban life know the boundaries that exist between relatively rich and relatively poor, white and black, older and younger, Manhattan and Brooklyn. The cultural distances are vast, and the boundaries between people are real. Joe's presence at our wedding was a sign that we together had crossed many social, economic, and racial boundaries that keep people apart, par-ticularly at festive events like weddings. When I ask myself why Joe came, the answer is very clear. Joe was present at this wedding because of the power of biblical storytelling in urban religious education. This is how that happened.

We had become close friends during Christmas vacation that

previous December. In my required religious education course at Union Theological Seminary, the professor required the class to design and carry out a specific educational project. I had been studying form criticism and oral tradition during my first Hebrew exegesis course on Exodus. Out of this, I designed a kind of oral tradition experience. I outlined the plan to the youth group and two signed on, Joe and Floyd. For five successive days between Christmas and New Year's day, I met with Joe and Floyd, for four hours a day! I look back on the experience now with amazement: Christmas vacation, three to four hours a day, two cool dude teenagers from Brooklyn and me learning and telling Bible stories! Incredible! It was my first experience in teaching biblical storytelling.

The memories of the process are not sharp and specific, but the outline is clear. We learned the stories around Moses's birth from Exodus 1 and 2 (the midwives, Moses' birth, and the murder of the overseer) and the stories of Jesus' birth from Luke 2. Each day we worked on another part of the story and Joe and Floyd were required to tell it to me the next day. After they had gotten through the story, I asked them what questions they had. In the process of learning the story each day, they came up with a significant number of questions. In each instance, we explored what the story had meant in its original historical context. We learned about slavery in the ancient Near East and the Egyptian pharaohs; we even went over to the Brooklyn Museum and looked at some of the Egyptian artifacts. I taught them a little Hebrew. We learned about the Roman Empire and the oppression of the Jews under Roman rule. And we looked at how these stories were related to the stories that preceded and followed them in the Bible.

Also each day I would ask them to tell stories from their own experience that were connected with these stories for them. Often it was necessary for me to help them identify the connections. Questions I would ask were: When have you had to hide in order to avoid being attacked by your enemies or be shrewd in order to get around decrees from authority figures? When have you gotten into a fight to defend your friends or been rejected or oppressed because of your racial identity? When have you found God present with you when you were

hurting? They told me stories about their experiences of discrimination and exclusion as young black men in the city. There
were stories about conflicts between gangs and the battle with
despair and drugs. They also told stories about the church and
how important it had been in supporting them in their struggles. As they told these stories from their own experience, the
stories from the Bible began to be more meaningful for them.
The sense of connection between their experience and the
births of Moses and Jesus and themselves gradually deepened
during the week. I also shared with them my experiences as a
white middle-class kid in a small town in southwestern Ohio.
We clearly came from very different worlds, but in the stories
we found a common ground that linked our stories together. By
the end of the week, we got to know each other well. We had
become close friends who shared common memories both
about God and about each other.

I know something happened, because otherwise Joe would
never have had the nerve to do what he did on my wedding
day. About an hour before the wedding as I was getting
dressed, Joe appeared at the door of my apartment. He helped
me get on my cummerbund and put the studs and cuff links in
the dress shirt. But during the whole time, he had one theme:
Kidding me as he would one of his contemporaries, he said,
"Tom, you don't have to do this. You are making a *big* mistake.
Go on, man, just leave. Get out of here." This teasing reflected
the depth of relationship that had been formed during our
months of biblical study together. We had formed a community
of memory composed of the stories of Israel in Egypt and of
Jesus' birth combined with our own experiences. Later, as an
inner-city pastor on the west side of Chicago, I heard black
storytelling preaching for the first time and came to recognize
the power of biblical storytelling. When biblical stories are
learned and told in connection with experience now, the power of God is often present. The more I have studied the development of ancient Israel and of the early church the more I am
convinced that storytelling was at the heart of their educational
system. Children were told the stories over and over and were
required to learn and tell them. In Jewish tradition, the bar
mitzvah is a continuation of that tradition in which a young

man, and now woman, stands and recites a story from the Hebrew scriptures to the congregation.

The early church was to a great degree an urban community. The church's principal development took place in the cities of the Hellenistic world. In that urban context, the most prevalent and powerful tradition was the broad-based storytelling tradition that resulted in the multifaceted narratives recorded in the four gospels. Everyone learned to tell a few stories. Storytelling was at the core of the overall religious education process. Children first heard the stories from parents and other members of the community, and then they were expected to learn to read and to tell the stories themselves. That was how they came to know God most deeply.

Well, Joe had learned the stories well. As we walked up the street, Joe, smiling like a Cheshire cat, got more urgent the closer we got to the chapel: "Tom, listen to me, remember the people of Israel. Escape, man. Just turn around and walk away from here. You're going to be a slave for life." I laughed and kept going. During the last block, he said, "Look, I'll cover for you. You just take off, and I'll tell them you got sick and had to go to the hospital. Or that you sent me to take your place. It doesn't matter; get out of here. Remember the people of Israel, slaves in Egypt. That's you as a married man! Go on, run." Not only had Joe memorized the stories, he could adapt them to contemporary situations!

The fact that Joe could give me such bachelor advice shows part of the value of the memorization that inevitably accompanies storytelling. In order to tell the story, you have to internalize it and make it your own. The value of storytelling is in part related to this process of internalization. One of the tragedies of contemporary religious education is the more or less exclusive association of memorization with rote repetition. In religious education, memorization of the Bible has been associated in recent centuries with learning individual verses to be used as proof texts. And when major parts of the church rejected the hermeneutic associated with proof texts, we also eliminated memorization of the biblical tradition from religious education. The tragedy is that we thereby eliminated a primary means for the internalization of the faith tradition. To a unique degree, religious education is related to remembering the acts of God and internalizing those memories in the deepest parts of ourselves. Thus, as with poetry and music, memorization is the first step in the resourcing of the imagination and the formation of the unconscious as well as the conscious mind. Joe was able to use the story imaginatively in this radically different context because he had internalized it.

Joe's tactics changed, but his tenacity did not end when we got to the chapel. He joined in encouraging people to sign the guest book, and his own name led the list. Joe, a highly sophisticated man, was able to move in many contexts with relative ease. But he also felt permission to enter into our celebration because he knew what we had shared. I now know that one of the gifts of the storytelling tradition is a unique power to form new communities.

Since then, the biblical storytelling tradition has been extended much more widely. There is now an extensive network of biblical storytellers in the United States that is rapidly becoming a worldwide network. Biblical stories have a unique capability to cut across the divisions that separate different cultures, racial groups, and economic classes. And within the storytelling matrix that is generated by these stories, everyone's story has a place.

At the heart of the process of religious education through storytelling is performance. Joe and Floyd came back each day in part because they liked to tell the stories. Like young people everywhere they learned stories with relative ease and responded warmly to the invitation and expectation that they tell the stories to someone else: to parents or grandparents, to young children or old folks, to the congregation, and to persons outside the parish. Performing provided a concrete motivation for learning the stories. Whether recomposed into raps or told in association with rock music, whether told with pictures or puppets, telling the stories of the actions of God is something that every child can do in some way. And, as in a Suzuki recital, the first responsibility of every adult who is present at any biblical storytelling event is to cheer and applaud.

The potential role of performance in the utilization of biblical storytelling in religious education has been most clearly developed in the work of Pamela Moffat, one of our earliest storyteller colleagues, now the associate minister at Trinity UCC in Miamisburg, Ohio, and executive director of the Network of Biblical Storytellers. The story which follows was written by Pam as an account of her experience when she made learning to tell the Gospel of Mark a major project for her youth group when she was an associate at a UCC church in Groton, Connecticut.

Pamela Moffat's Story

"The past five years of my ministry have been based on teaching, telling, and sharing with others the story of our faith in Mark's gospel. In the early days of my ministry, I recognized the power the word had when it was shared as story. However, I also found that people had a very low tolerance level for memorizing the story as a story. It reeked of school and reminded people of all their failings at 'learning' facts and figures. There had to be a medium which would empower the people with the biblical story in order to allow it to shape and form their own life story.

"Working with the youth of the First Church of Christ, Congregational, in Groton, Connecticut, I noticed that music was the major medium both for learning and for the formation of value judgments. The kids only had to hear a song two or three times before they were capable of singing along with the record. By the time they had heard it another two or three times, they were humming or singing the words with the music at a very subconscious level. I decided that if I were able to capitalize on this learning pattern, I could give them a life-shaping story which would be with them for the rest of their lives.

"Steve Rose offered his God-given gift of being able to transcribe printed words into song—songs which were easily learned, tunes which were easily remembered. He set major parts of the Gospel of Mark to music. The process of building a strong biblical base in the lives of many young people had begun!

"Due to my absolute ignorance of musical theory or practice, and without being able to read one note of music, I embarked on a blind journey of faith with thirty young people, aged twelve to eighteen. We listened to very rough tapes which Steve sent, singing along with him over and over and over again. (In fact, the tapes were so rough that when he would stop mid-verse to change a word or the tune, the kids in the re-singing would stop and make the same changes with him— even after we left the tapes behind and began singing them on our own!) After the first week of listening to the tapes, both as a group and at home, we knew, in a way that could never be taken away from us, at least the equivalent of four chapters of Mark's gospel. It became clear to us and to those who knew what we were doing that the Spirit was alive and active in our lives. Further, it gave us a common base for our questions both about life and about God. Counseling and contacts with the kids and their families became a joy because we knew where each other was grounded—in the biblical story of salvation of which we were a part.

"For the next three months we worked on learning the parts of the story which the songs did not cover and on refining the words and the music. We then had to decide how we were going to share the story with others. We decided we would "perform" the Gospel of Mark from Chapter 1 verse 1 through the Transfiguration, ending at Chapter 9, verse 8.

"At the end of the summer, we went to camp for a week. We worked on the stories while we were swimming, eating, and canoeing from dawn until late at night. One night we had a campfire at which we sang and told everything that we had learned from the Gospel of Mark. The lake where we were camping was a large lake with a number of campsites around it. We had seen a number of people at various points but had not interacted with any of them other than exchanging civilities. As we were singing and telling the stories, we couldn't see a thing because of our campfire. But, when we stopped singing at one point, we suddenly heard applause echoing across the lake. The kids were so excited that they started yelling for the people to come and join us. They came from all over the lake, some walking and some in cars. Those in cars surrounded the campfire. And we sang the rest of the gospel for them.

"The people stayed until late that night. And they were so appreciative that the kids couldn't believe it. From then on, there was no stopping them.

"The end product which we wanted to share with the out-side world was neither professional nor original. Rather it was our gift to those who came to listen and to watch. The power of the story was conveyed through the expressions in the eyes of the kids and the sincerity of their presentation rather than through the quality of the voices or the acting ability of the youth. Everyone knew that the kids believed what they shared. We traveled through Connecticut and Pennsylvania sharing the power of God's gift to us in the story of Jesus' life and ministry as it was recorded for us in Mark's gospel and as it shone through us in our telling.

"I am convinced that it was through the medium of music that the story became alive and met the youth where they were. The music and the story together created a context in which God was able to enter into the lives of both the tellers and the listeners.

"Since that first experience, my entire ministry has been grounded in the telling and teaching of the biblical story. I have conducted two week-long summer conferences for the Con-necticut Conference of the United Church of Christ for junior high students in which over 120 youth have learned the entire Gospel of Mark from the RSV. The response has been over-whelming from the home churches as well as from the youth who have been involved. I have also conducted workshops on the Gospel of Mark in music for the United Methodist Church. They were received as welcome beginning points for the reap-propriation of the biblical tradition in the education ministry of the local church. At the present time, I am involved in leading workshops which are designed to enable youth leaders to use the materials on the Gospel of Mark on their own."

Some Concluding Observations

The importance of this experience is its demonstration of the potential of biblical storytelling to provide a center for the religious education of youth. Undoubtedly, the development of the music has been a crucial element in making this program possible. And it is doubtful that the storytelling process would have this degree of meaning without the music.

However, in her religious education program with children, Pam has developed a storytelling curriculum in which the teachers have learned to tell the stories without the assistance of folk music. Thus, while the music has been central to the development of the youth program, the overall religious education program has also been significantly enhanced through the telling of the stories. But, in relation to the youth, the motivation to learn the stories has been the prospect of telling them to people outside the local congregation. Both the challenge and the promise of that mission has given them a reason to learn.

Out of this experience with the gospel, the youth became involved in a variety of social action projects: a soup kitchen, visiting youth in prison and on drugs, collecting and distributing clothing for needy families, and the support of a mission project in Haiti. Thus, through learning to tell the stories of the Gospel of Mark, these young people internalized the stories and lived them out in action. In this project, the marks of the original medium of biblical narrative were present: the experience of the gospel in sound, the memorization and internalization of the stories, the formation of community, and the initiation and development of a storytelling network which reaches out beyond the community to others in need. Pamela's project is one of many that have grown out of that initial storytelling experience with Joe and Floyd. Now the learning and telling of the stories has become a widely used resource for religious education throughout the world.

I feel good about what I taught Joe and what happened in our relationship. I know our time to teach children and youth about God is very limited. It strikes me as wise that the limited time we have should be significantly devoted to telling and learning the stories of the acts of God in Israel and through Jesus Christ. We can teach the foundational stories and encourage students to learn them deeply. And what will they remember? They will remember moments of intimacy and love, moments when the ancient stories about God somehow connected with their own lives and experience. Those memories will help form the matrix for new relationships and new communities.

The basic steps in learning biblical stories are easy and natural: mastery/memorization, study of the story in its original historical context, internalization and appropriation of the story in relation to present experience, and telling the story. As with dance, from these basic steps, all sorts of innovations and improvisations are possible. The key is to listen for the reality of God then and now. When that listening is steady and deep, the voice of God will be heard. In some way, God will speak to the community and to each person. The responses will also vary, and it is essential to preserve the freedom to respond in a variety of ways.

The streets are places of oral tradition. When the word about something goes out on the streets, it gets around fast. Learning how to teach in urban churches is connected with learning how to relate to the oral networks and the vibes of the neighborhood. There is no more natural or powerful resource for urban religious education than telling and enabling young people to learn to tell the stories of the Bible.

Chapter 14

Two Weekday Alternatives in Urban Religious Education

The Released Time Model

Terry Heck

The title for the first part of this chapter could be, "The Overlooked Open Door" as prompted by a publication of the Center for Law and Religious Freedom of the Christian Legal Society. The next few pages identify the opportunity for using Weekday Religious Education/Released Time (shortened to WDRE/RT for this chapter) in the urban setting. This model is one of the real, although currently neglected, valuable opportunities for urban churches to partially fulfull their religious education mandates.

Weekday Religious Education/Released Time is a program in which participating children, with their parents' consent, are either released early from school or directly after school to go to a nearby church for religious instruction. In this way, religious education is made available to public school children.

The traditional forms of Sunday-based religious education in urban churches run into some problems that the WDRE/RT programs can overcome, such as leadership, outreach, and motivation. In some urban churches, education leadership is a real issue. A WDRE/RT program is advantageous to the urban church because its cooperative institutional recruitment and financial support makes recruitment of a volunteer or employment of a professional teacher an easier task. WDRE/RT programs are attractive to leadership because in them the religious education is conducted in its own special time frame, rather than as an offshoot of a busy Sunday morning.

Released time is also useful to the urban church because it is a means of relevant and effective outreach. The fact that, by far, most of the children involved in these programs have no church affiliation, indicates the outreach potential. WDRE/RT programs make religious education look attractive. Some children will become involved out of curiosity and will stay. The fact that children attend the program with their peers and schoolmates increases the likelihood of student-initiated outreach and reinforcement. In urban settings the peer group is a potent force.

In most situations the ease of getting from the school to the church is a major factor. While some churches will supply bus assistance for bringing the children from the school to the church, and/or taking the children home from the church if they are already involved in bus transportation to public school, in most instances the task is only a matter of walking with the teacher and parental supervisor from school to church. This makes this pattern a very useful one in the urban setting.

Though WDRE/RT is definitely legal,[1] nonetheless some urban communities have been hesitant to adopt it. The cooperation of the local school board and various administrators is crucial to the program's success.

Once very popular, the WDRE/RT program is experiencing a renewal of interest based on a new realization of its great potential. The first such programs began in the United States around 1914. One begun by School Superintendent William Wirt and area pastors in Gary, Indiana, was the program recognized as first in the Golden Anniversary Celebration of 1964. WDRE/RT was seen then within the framework of Adelaide Case's definition of Christian religious education to the effect that we intend to share with the present generation — children, youth, and adults — the accumulated riches of the Christian faith in such a way that God in Christ may work in each human soul and in the common life of humanity. The program grew to a peak in the early 1950s when it is estimated that there were programs in 3,000 communities with an enrollment of 2,250,000.

A shift to social action concerns, civil rights, and war issues in the 1960s, coupled with confusion regarding church-state relationships fostered a decline. But in 1982, a national consultation was held. Ten states and the District of Columbia were represented. A good cross section of interest was displayed, as well, by the presence of representatives from the National Council of Churches, state and local councils, Roman Catholic educational leaders, evangelical Christian groups in the sphere of the National Association of Evangelicals, the nondenominational Bible Club Movement, and the Children's Bible Mission. Denominationally those in the consultation were related to the Roman Catholic Church, the Greek Orthodox Church, the Southern Baptist Churches, the United Methodist Church, the United Church of Christ, the Christian Church (Disciples of Christ), the American Lutheran Church, the North American Convention of Christian Churches, the Plymouth Brethren, United Brethren in Christ, Mennonite (General Conference), the Missionary Church, Christian Methodist Episcopal Church, Progressive National Baptist Convention, Bible Baptist, Independent Baptist, and independent, nondenominational churches.

Here is the way one urban congregation portrays their involvement in WDRE/RT: "We are working with the children of our church's service area, so we have a vested interest," said Sharon Jones, director of the church's program. "We have been able to share the problems of our children and their families and provide a support system for them. There have even been times when the schools have called to alert us to problems with which they thought we could help."[2]

Jones said the congregation began its released time program three years ago. With assistance from Terry Heck, who served as a consultant, Jones led the church in developing its own curriculum and making sure the program did not violate civil law.

Jones visited the principals of the two elementary schools to ask their permission in releasing the second, third, and fourth graders who would be participating in the program. "The better the relationship between the principals and the released time personnel, the better the program is," she said. Next, Jones and church volunteers handed out parental permission slips to the children as they left school property in the afternoon.

Children who join the program are met by a volunteer at the school and taken to the nearby church on foot or by bus. There they participate in an hour and a half of varied educational activities. They are then assisted in the appropriate ways to their homes. The program, which began with 50 students during its first year, now has reached its maximum of 115 students. Of those students, Jones said, only one-fourth have any church affiliation. "Even though the parents don't go to church," she said, "they recognize the need for their children to know about God."

Since the program's inception, more than twenty families have joined the church as a result of their children's participation. Although the program avoids teaching Baptist doctrine—it emphasizes an ecumenical stance, teaching general concepts about God and Jesus—Jones said the church regularly sends letters to the children's families inviting them to various church activities.

The program planners hold to these guidelines:

1. Make sure the program fulfills legal requirements. Remember that the sponsor, not the school, has to do the work.

2. Build relationships with the schools and school boards. Few states require schools to release students.

3. Develop a broad-based support group for the program. Programs that appeal to a wide range of church affiliations are preferable.

4. Do not make students who do not participate in the program feel ostracized.

Most religious education programs eventually develop their own curricular resources or make adaptations of existing materials. Ruth Correll in a 1978 survey found a wide range of materials being used.[3]

Just as the resources used vary, so do program formats. Not every program looks the same. These differences of approach and administration can be seen in a comparison of a Roman

Catholic, a Protestant, and a Jewish program.

Roman Catholic: In this program, the parochial school dismisses one hour early on Wednesday afternoon so that children from the nearby public schools may walk to WDRE/RT classes in the parochial school. Since the parish serves a specific geographic area, transportation is not a problem. There are about two classes for each grade level, averaging twenty-five children each. The CCD curriculum is used serving grades 2-4 plus a class for Italian-speaking children. Children are interviewed individually before first penance and first communion regarding their understanding of the Ten Commandments and other concepts taught.

Being aware that WDRE/RT is the only religious education of children this age, the parish is very supportive of the program. Parents pay a registration fee in the fall of only $15 for one child or $20 for more than one. Some teachers are parents or other volunteers, and others teach WDRE/RT under their contracts as teachers in the parochial school. Excellent rapport exists among the faculty and children, and teachers enjoy refreshments and conversation after class in the office. This is a generally very enjoyable, enthusiastic, and well-attended program involving many people in the parish. WDRE/RT has long been established in this Brooklyn community.

Protestant: This small Queens congregation's Sunday school began to dwindle, and volunteer teachers were difficult to recruit for the time during the worship service. In 1965, the parish decided to switch to WDRE/RT for religious education. Classes meet from 2:00-4:00 P.M. on Wednesday with a class of four to five children in each grade, totaling twenty-five. At first, the *Christian Faith and Life* series was used, but volunteer religious educators found David C. Cook Co. materials more suited to their needs. Now they plan to change to the new ecumenical *Christian Education: Shared Approaches* curriculum. Most of the religion teachers are parent volunteers.

No tuition is charged, but a special Mother's Day offering and weekly children's offerings help support the program. A full 50 percent of the children who attend are not from the congregation, and a nearby church of another denomination encourages its children to attend. Some Roman Catholic children come until their own CCD classes begin. Children in WDRE/RT are involved in regular parish worship in a monthly choir anthem and as acolytes and as particpants in quarterly evening game nights. Twice a year, the children lead the worship service. The two-hour period and small classes permit close relationships to develop for prayer and fellowship among students and teachers.

Jewish: This Conservative Jewish congregation has a six-hour religious education program which meets after school for two hours, three days per week. By using the WDRE/RT hour on Wednesday, children can get home an hour earlier that day. Bus transportation provided by the Community Center brings children from surrounding schools. Children must attend these classes (averaging twenty) beginning in third or fourth grade to be *Bar Mitzvah*.

Parents pay tuition ($135 member; $260 nonmember) for the total program. The congregation underwrites 35 percent of the budget. Teachers are fully trained for this program and teach half-time at a professional rate of pay. A parallel program for parents is available at the Center, and a strong parent organization provides prizes for excellence in achievement.

The Melton Research Center provides materials as a pilot project of Jewish Theological Seminary and a consortium from Hebrew University in Jerusalem. The classes emphasize learning Hebrew well enough to get meaning from the text, Jewish history, Jewish practices, and readings from the Bible by sixth grade. This is an excellent academic program, well-designed, and seriously accepted and respected by the Conservative Jewish community.

The Supplementary Christian School

Nellie Metz

Another approach to school-related religious education that differs somewhat from the WDRE/RT has been developed by Nellie Metz, and is called the Supplementary Christian School

(SCS). It is an extension of the school day in a learning laboratory in a church or a non-school designated building, where the Bible and other religious materials are used as the texts. A supplementary individualized curriculum is planned and taught by certificated educators with volunteer assistants who provide children with beneficial individualized tutoring in general education skills.

Supplementary Christian Schools are of special benefit in the urban setting. Many urban schools are overcrowded and understaffed. Sometimes funds for remedial or enrichment programs are not available, and private tutoring is expensive. Parents who recognize their children's special needs cannot do the tutoring themselves and are reluctant or unable to place their children in a private situation where that supplementary attention might be given.

The SCS combines the Christian philosophy of attention to individual needs with Christian content via biblical and other religious materials as it tutors children in general education skills. The SCS is a very practical application of religious education.

Children and youth in a program such as this receive several benefits: 1) the reinforcement of learning skills, 2) greater familiarity with the Bible and other religious materials, and 3) a challenge to reach a fuller potential. The SCS program helps those children, for example, who develop negative attitudes toward learning, school, and themselves because they are unable to read up to grade level. The public school is not always able to meet that individual need and is prohibited by law from teaching religion in a way some parents would like. Sunday school teachers and CCD religious educators, on the other hand, have too little time in most program settings and are not trained to recognize and respond to the individual needs. Thus too many children experience unnecessary negative feelings. The SCS enables the children to continue to attend the public school and also receive the added benefit of a Christian school.

A Supplementary Christian School differs from a WDRE/RT in these ways: It operates on an after-school, Saturday, and summer vacation model. It focuses upon children whose parents are more apt to be active members of churches and want this kind of assistance for their children in a religious context. It seeks to be directly related to general education learning skills.

An SCS can be as large or small as a church or group of churches want to make it. The minimum requirement in this model is one certificated teacher. That requirement is based upon the desire to have the close interaction with the public school staff and the need for careful development of the individualized curriculum. The SCS could be expanded to many grade levels, with added staff such as guidance counselors, psychologists, and learning disability experts.

Here is a sample plan that gives an idea of the type of schedule that could be developed:

Terms—three six-week terms—fall, winter, spring, with eighteen hours of instruction each term. Grades K-3 could meet Mondays and Wednesdays; grades 4-6 could meet Tuesdays and Thursdays; all grades could meet also on Saturdays for an extended session where special supplementary lessons might be offered in music in addition to the general education work. Two three-week summer terms would complete the plan for a year.

The program is conceived as placing an emphasis on these "Three R's": Remediation (helping the child in weak academic areas); Reinforcement (giving encouragement in the accomplishment of skills); and enRichment (challenging children in areas of giftedness).

The curriculum, planned by the religious education administrator and staff, would center around religious themes and topics, making heavy use of religious materials and being guided by the knowledge of the individual child's needs. Diagnostic testing or the determination of those needs through the conversation with the public school staff (parental permission having been granted) is critical in this model. These academic/general education needs of each child are then worked on within the religion curriculum.

The SCS meets the needs of urban children and youth at basic and important levels. It provides that individualized attention and tutoring that can help each child reach his or her full potential as a child of God. It increases literacy, one of the keys necessary to fuller understanding of the gospel. It increases the child's chances of economic success after schooling is finished. It provides a caring climate where self-worth is affirmed and where Christian friendships can develop. Over all, it blends content and method, integrating Christian teachings and Christ-like teaching in a program that testifies to God's involvement in the world.

What these two models have in common is some relation-ship to the public school experience of the child. Both often depend upon specially trained and employed staff. The one, WDRE/RT, has the particular value of providing education in religion to children and youth who might not otherwise have any such opportunity. The other, SCS, teaches the Bible and other religious materials in an education ministry that assists children in general learning skills. Both are successful alterna-tives to a Sunday-based religious education program.

Notes

1. In the case of *Smith v. Smith* decided January 19, 1976, the U.S. Supreme Court upheld the policy of a school board's releasing stu-dents from school for religious instruction off school grounds while other students remained in the classroom and did not receive formal instruction. Released time for religious instruction off school grounds but during school hours has been accepted by the United States Supreme Court as constitutionally permissible. See *Zorak v. Clauson*, 343 U.S. 306, 72 S. Ct. 679, 96 L.Ed. 954 (1952).

2. Correspondence to the author.

3. *Footsteps of Faith* by Bible Club Movement - 8 year (4 Old Testament, 4 New Testament) through the Bible survey. Emphasizes flannelgraph Bible story, Bible drills, and memory verses with tokens for achievement which may earn a child a free week at camp in the summer.

Through-the-Week adapted by the National Council of Churches in conjunction with various pilot projects approved by sponsoring com-mittees.

Child Evangelism Fellowship series - 6 year cycle: Lives of Patriarchs; Moses and the Tabernacle; Joshua, Judges, and David; Elijah, Elisha, and God Word; Life of Christ; and Acts. Format is similar to BCM above.

The Greatest Book in Pictures by Released Time in Sacramento, CA - grades 4-6 in 3 series: Book of Beginnings, Patriarchs, and Seven Bible

Themes; Old Testament through the division of the kingdom, and Life of Christ. Memorized selections are usually longer passages than in other materials, such as, for example, the Ten Commandments and the 23rd Psalm.

Gift by Winston Press, a Roman Catholic publishing house in Minneapolis.

Plus supplementary programs used in high school situations as electives in Social Studies courses (Bible survey, great Christians, denominational histories, values clarification, life adjustment, and the like).

Chapter 15

Out of the City/Into the City: Two Camping Models for the Urban Church

Action Planning the Urban Camping Excursion

Richard L. Stackpole

The unique power of camping for the shaping of lives after the pattern of Christ is well-known and firmly established. The "time-away" in a different environment allows a fresh perspective on self and God. The relative increase in the intensification of interpersonal contacts brought about by a total experience of twenty-four-hour-a-day for six days also puts things in a new light. Sometimes the unpredicted events of small-group living bring lessons of life and scripture to the fore with a particularly profound relevance. All of this is known, as are the opportunities to experience the new and the challenging and the nurturing of deepened friendships.

There are, of course, urban populations for whom camping is a long-established and accepted activity. The fact that some urban youth and children and adults go camping is no different from the procedures and expectations that characterize much church camping. But for some camping is not a familiar experience, and that more rustic camping environment is not familiar turf. This chapter addresses the issues that arise when camping with urban youth is new to an urban community.

Camping is a means to an end, and not an end in itself. Camping is a resource that can be utilized by the local urban church to enhance its overall work.

URBAN CAMP. . . . WHAT IS IT?

Urban camp is a camp experience shared by urban youth. Two groups that may receive special benefit from a successful camping experience are urban minority youth and children. These children or youth may come from an underprivileged economic setting and may have experienced the problem of discrimination throughout their lives. The urban camping experience can provide them with a setting and a program that breaks down the barriers of their economic and racial depressions, can bring them a sense of acceptance in a Christian community and of responsibility to and for each individual within that community, and can give them a sense of personal achievement in an environment that is generally foreign to them—the "wilderness." This experience helps equip them to carry from the wilderness setting back to the urban setting an enhanced sense of community acceptance, responsibility, and personal self-esteem. The urban camp experience can and does give such experiences to urban minority youth.

ACTION PLANNING: BEGINNINGS

When I take a group of urban youth camping, I deliberately and consciously plan for success. First, I gather together skilled adults in my church or community who have an interest in youth and in this sort of event. The pastor, religious educators, activity directors, public school teachers—these people have backgrounds and skills that can be brought together into a "steering committee" which actually plans the event. Second, I make sure I have the support of my church or organization. Such support sounds like a given, but it is important to have that support, enthusiastically as well as financially, from the beginning. Financial support is essential. Many, if not most, of the target group of youth would be unable to afford a week's experience at camp without such support from the local church, from the larger judicatory body of the denomination, or from suburban and rural churches willing to reach out and help their urban brothers and sisters. It is also vitally important to recruit counselors for the experience as soon as possible and bring them into the planning stage.

"Get Ready": Goals and Objectives

The first responsibility of the steering committee in planning an urban camp is the development of a goal. The goal is a general statement of intent, and is used as a measure for all activities and events planned for the experience, taking each activity or event and asking, in the planning stage, "Does this help us to achieve our goal with the urban youth we are going to be working with?" For example, a goal might be stated as follows: "To create a wilderness community that stresses the enhancement of self-concept and personal responsibility within a community setting."

The second responsibility of the steering committee is planning objectives. Objectives are the specifics. These are the defined activities and events planned for the urban camping experience which will assist in achieving the goal. For example:

A. Provide an enriching experience for urban minorities in a setting beyond the city, an accepting Christian community setting with the wilderness creating a common denominator between all members of the community, a living experience which relates a group of eight youth and two adults together for five days stressing:

1. Relational skill building;
2. Appropriate understandings of personal responsibility in a group;
3. Sharing;
4. Group consensus decision making;
5. Group development and involvement through noncompetitive gaming;
6. Respect for property and personal belongings.

B. Development of self-esteem through exposure to and skill development in such outdoor living skills as:

1. Cooking;
2. Campcrafts: rope lashing, safe usage of common camp tools;

3. Environmental acclimatizing;
4. Responsibility for the environment with minimum impacting;
C. Development of self-esteem through modest risk situations, such as:
1. Swimming lessons;
2. Basic life saving and water safety;
3. Canoeing and rowboating;
D. Increase the camper's identification with his or her local church and the church's place in his or her urban setting.

Each of the previous examples addresses one or more areas of the general goal developed for the urban camp experience.

In planning the time together with the urban children and youth, it is essential to begin with the goal and objectives. In this way we are forcing ourselves to put together a well-thought-out event and know from the beginning where we want to head with the plans. Also, the goal and the specific objectives are excellent tools for evaluation of the event afterwards when we can ask, "Okay, did we achieve this during our time in the camp experience?" Remember to have in mind a specific site during this early planning stage and bring in a representative from that camping facility to assist you in developing your specifics, your objectives. This person will be able to point out the activities that are appropriate for the experience and what resources are available, both in terms of tools and facilities and with the wilderness environment itself.

From these initial steps, setting goals and objectives, the steering committee needs to address other basic issues:

Counselor Training. Who and how to train? (Discussed.)

Age Level. Be careful here. Grouping seven-year-olds and eleven-year-olds together can be disastrous! Keep the age span within a year or so, such as nine- to eleven-year-olds. Do not stray from this decision. The developmental stages of children vary widely, making the development of a curriculum for a large age span nearly impossible. Similarly the approaches to teaching, discipline, skill abilities, social development, and participation would all be unnecessarily cumbersome.

Adult/Child Ratios. These are largely dependent upon the state laws and the rules of the camp facility. I would suggest one adult per four youth to be the highest ratio for preteens and teens. A one-to-three or less is best for younger children. The more one-on-one attention with the youth, who find themselves in a foreign and threatening environment, the better.

Family Groups. This is one of the best approaches to camping with urban young people. The family group is a child's identity group. It consists of one male and one female counselor, and an even balance of boys and girls. This small-group approach creates a true sense of family, filled with all the joyful and painful experiences found in a family. It also is a vehicle for achieving your goal of developing a sense of Christian community, if you choose such a goal. Remember that a caring community setting is foreign to some urban children and youth. It will take a while for them to test out the safety of this new situation. Be patient! You may see great things happen by the end of your stay at camp.

Curriculum. One of our primary concerns in developing a curriculum was the matter of illiteracy among urban children and youth. We addressed this issue by utilizing counselor-led oral instruction. Instead of working with a reading hand-out to the campers, we found that preparing the counselors beforehand with their own handbooks of curriculum resources worked well. In the counselor handbook were activities to do as a group, scripture readings, and stories to tell, all grouped into topic areas dealing with specific objectives for the week: Ego Enrichment, Acceptance of Others, Problem Resolution, Community Living. There is a freedom here for the counselor in observing what the family group needs and addressing each situation appropriately out of the handbook of resources. Yet at the same time there should be a structure to the curriculum. At the very least, have a daily theme, with each day building on the previous day. Such as: Day One—I am someone; Day Two—You are someone; Day Three—We are a family; Day Four—We are a family of God.

Christianity has a rich heritage in the oral tradition and transmission of the good news. By relating to the urban campers in this way, and avoiding having *them* read, you avoid the trap of making camp feel like or sound like school. Many urban youth, of course, have not had great success in school. The counselor is the primary curriculum resource. The rationale behind this approach is that the counselor is given a large amount of freedom with the campers, allowing for an openness to address what is current with the group and fostering the "teachable moment," that precious time of spontaneity. Equipping the counselor is essential with this approach. Don't ask them to read a couple of passages and then go to camp! Prepare them for each day's theme.

One final thought about the oral tradition. Often times storytelling involves interpreting a scriptural passage or parable in a modern-day fashion. Be aware of the religious background of the youth. For some urban youth with a more literal interpretation in their background, a strict retelling might be better than a modern interpretation.

"Get Set": Counselor Training

During the process of defining what you want your urban camp to be (the goal) and how specifically you are going to achieve the goal (the objectives), it is important to begin gathering a staff for the experience. Included in the staff are the camp dean or director, the resource people, and the counselors. The dean is the overseer. This person does not have specific responsibilities regarding the youth coming to the camp. Rather, the dean's responsibility is to the counselors—training them, assisting them during the week by helping them focus on the goal and objectives, addressing specific problems that arise, matching needs that come up with resources that are available, and leading the post-camp evaluation. The resource people should be those from the church or community group, along with staff people from the camp facility, who have specific skills that will enhance the experience: people with experience in crafts, gaming, campfire singing, swimming, boating, etc. (depending on the objectives).

The third group, and the most important for the event, are the counselors. These are the people who become intimately involved with the urban children and youth during the time at camp. We have found that the best counselors are those who already know the youth going to camp. The reason for this is that people familiar with the specific youth tend to have a better understanding of their backgrounds and the details of their family life. With this knowledge, they are better equipped to address the "baggage," or personal experiences and agendas, that the campers bring to the camp. Once the counselors have been chosen, a well-planned counselor training period will insure a good experience at camp for everyone. Here are some suggestions for that training period:

1. A clear understanding of the goal and objectives. Are they understood? Are the concrete plans for achieving them clear and within reach of the counselor?

2. Clearly defined responsibilities. The camp facility representative can help here. What are the rules imposed by the state for a camping experience? For example, all campers must be within voice-range of the counselor at all times; the counselor must be able to locate each camper in his or her care at all times; the counselor is to stay with the campers during the evening and not leave them on their own in the cabins or tents. The counselor should make these "imposed" responsibilities very clear; perhaps even point out the legal and liability ramifications. What are the responsibilities expected by the camp facility? No running in certain areas; everyone remains at the dinner table until the group is dismissed; certain wilderness areas are off-limits; a certain adult/youth ratio must be maintained at all times. Again, the camp facility representative is the best resource in clarifying these important matters.

3. Clear expectations. Counselors should be trained so they know what can be expected to happen in specific camp areas? The director should review with the counselors *every* area where campers will be involved.

The counselors should consider the following:

The *Sleeping Area*. The counselors should imagine potential dynamics that can take place here: camper's needs during the first night as they get used to a foreign and threatening new world; the objectives during the quiet time; setting down the law in the cabin or tent; settling in for the night—using storytelling and singing right away to focus attention and interest. Also, the counselors should explore the physical arrangements of the sleeping area. The counselor will want to place himself or herself near the exit, staying alert at night for campers sneaking out or walking out in a sleep-walking state!

The *Trails*. Imagine the dynamics here: the danger areas; plan trail games to play; songs to sing in line; reciting the oral tradition (scripture) as "rap" or "jingle." Remember, one counselor will be in front of the line and one behind, with the rear counselor always in sight of the front counselor.

Nature. Urban campers usually do better with just experiencing the world around them rather than learning specific academia. Thus the counselor should not worry about naming trees and being sure to explain biological terms. The counselor should point out examples of cooperation taking place in the woods, the field, the pond. Relate those examples to cooperation in the group, and in the urban community at home. The counselor will be pleased with the insights that these children will come up with when they "expand their horizons." The camp facility's environmentalist will be a great resource here. Also, many urban campers come with the belief that spiders and cicadas are bad, and some are terrified of creepy-crawly things! Once the urban campers begin to sense the range of creation, they begin to realize they do not have to "stomp" on things just because they do not like them! Finally, the counselor should realize that the sounds of the wilderness are completely foreign to urban youth. They may be frightened by the sound of a hoot-owl. Help them to feel secure in their new world.

Home-in-the-woods. A home-in-the-woods is a special place for the urban camper's family group. It is a place away from the central campsite that the family group has chosen as their own during their stay at camp. Here is where a great amount of time can be spent working together lashing a lean-to, gathering wood, building a campfire, singing and sharing, teaching and learning. Own and respect that home. The counselor should be warm and foster open sharing there. Additionally, the counselor ought to be intentional in what they do as a group to build and maintain their woods home (campcraft skill development). Make sure campers have responsibilities that call them to participate with the family group. Cookouts in the home-in-the-woods are valuable times. Campers not only learn and enhance campcraft skills but develop a sense of self-support unlike any situation they have ever encountered.

The *Waterfront*. Safety first, involvement second! As a counselor, expect to get wet, to teach, to row, to paddle, to have fun. If the counselor doesn't get wet, then he or she should not expect the urban kids to get wet either.

The *Dining Hall* (or eating area). At his or her own table, the counselor must stress table manners, eating habits, and good nutrition. The counselor should likewise be alert to his or her own table manners. If the counselor begins the week by deprecating the food as "yucky" or by wasting food, the counselor has already lost the battle with the campers for the rest of the week. The counselor has to set the rules down early and stick to them: Ask and don't reach, try each dish (even with a "no-thank-you" helping), stay seated (and seated means sitting on your fanny, not standing or kneeling in the chair!), stay at your table until the entire group is dismissed. Planning meals usually is the responsibility of the camp staff, not the counselor. Nonetheless the counselor should be aware of certain attitudes that urban youth sometimes bring to camp regarding food. Some youngsters may have been told at home that certain things are not good to eat; some have looked forward to grits instead of cream of wheat; others may devour the fresh fruit! With a basic knowledge of the campers beforehand, you can help the camp kitchen staff with suggestions along these lines.

Discipline. What does the counselor do when someone breaks a rule? It will happen, so the counselors should anticipate the rebellious spirit they will encounter! Someone might get into someone else's "stuff," or two kids might get into a fist fight. Whatever the situation is, the counselor will have to address discipline. Before camp starts is the time to set the approach to this. The counselor would do well to use some form of discipline that avoids any violent reaction in the kids. Campers know violent forms of punishment all too well (and this is not particular to just urban children and youth!). Counselors should not, under any circumstance, physically punish a child in a violent manner. Brainstorm alternative forms of punishment. One we came up with was "time-out." When a child misbehaves, the counselor should remove a "reward activity" from that child. Most campers love swimming and gaming. Sitting out during a swim period or game time is a good punishment. The counselor should explain *why* they are being punished and point out that they are still loved and appreciated, but their behavior in that instance is what is not liked! One of my own first-year counselors put this most succinctly: "Urban camp gave us an opportunity to model and live out Christianity. I think this was one of the most positive things to happen. Young people saw that adults who were Christian respond differently than they often experienced in their lives. When somebody hit, it wasn't expected that they would be hit back."

The camp director ought not stop with this small list of expectations. The director should brainstorm with the counselors on what else they are concerned about and how the staff will approach those issues. Ask: Where are other times we work in our small family group setting and what should we expect, how can we prepare?

"Go": The Urban Camper

We have planned the camp event. We have trained the counselors. At this point we have gathered a group of youth from the church or organization to go to camp. Are *they* ready? Are the campers ready? The following thoughts are ideas to help prepare the urban youth for a camping experience.

Pre-camp preparation. A gathering of the kids and counselors should be convened within a month prior to the event. If possible, a representative from the camp facility should come to this gathering to share with the urban children and your youth thoughts and ideas about camping in general and the camp facility. If the camp representative has a slide show or videotape that will give visual exposure to the camp, especially the areas where the campers will be active, present that at this time. If not, a camp counselor or central staff person should go to the camp facility beforehand and take slide pictures to show. Everything should be done to increase the child's familiarity with the facility and with the counselors during the pre-camp activity.

What to bring. Urban children and youth should be assisted in deciding what they are to bring to camp. The best way to do this is have the counselors in charge of each family group visit the homes of those children and help gather what is needed. Basically, each camper should bring enough clothes (warm weather and cool weather) for the event, a sleeping bag and pillow (some families are not be able to afford sleeping bags and will send their camper to camp with a sheet and no blanket; assist them here), toiletries (toothbrush, toothpaste, shampoo), two pair of sneakers (or an extra pair of hiking shoes), a bathing suit and towel, and whatever else they need based on your objectives. It should always be borne in mind that many urban kids are poor and cannot afford many camp supplies. In such cases, the church should help out where needed. Putting together "Care Packages" of soap, shampoo, is an easy way for the local church to be more fully involved in its urban camp program.

What not to bring. These suggestions help cut down on problems that can arise during time at camp. NO: radio/cassette players, drugs, alcohol, tobacco products, knives, etc. Also, no extra cash. If there is a camp store a system should be prearranged in which each camper will have a "tab," a set amount of money set aside and already given to the camp to purchase store items. This way, problems of stealing or losing money will be avoided, together with all the blaming and hard feelings that go along with such.

Once at the camp facility, there are a couple of ground rules to set down within the first day.

Rules. Have rules pre-planned. Trying to have the campers create their own rules generally does not work in the camp setting. This is because most of these urban young people have never previously experienced something like camp and so really do not know what to expect. The rules as means of maintaining safety should be carefully explained to the campers. This approach opens them up to the rules better and also tells them that counselors and central staff are there for their safety and that you care about them. Also, if youngsters feel they are in a safe situation they are more apt to try out new things. Some suggested rules: interpersonal rules (no put-downs, stay out of other's belongings), dinner table rules, bathroom rules.

Orientation. In the first few hours, the campers should be taken for a walk around the camp facilities. Counselors should point out both what the campers will be doing in those places and the safety rules specific to those areas. During both the rules and orientation periods, the counselors should keep things short and to the point, remembering the attention-span of the age group.

After all these vital preliminaries, the time comes to have fun and enjoy the experience of Christ and nature together with the campers, learning about cooperation and love and forgiveness and building self-esteem.

The following pointers and suggestions should be of additional assistance in enhancing the success of the urban camp experience. These pointers are things which my camp staff and I have learned in our own urban camp ministry.

Rest for the counselors. If possible, utilize the central staff at times for large-group events, such as gaming or campfires, so that the counselors can get away and have some time to themselves. Counselors are people too, and need this "battery recharging" time, especially as the week wears on. Such rest and recharging should be built into the schedule.

Graffiti. Kids need to "leave their mark." If they do this all over the camp facilities, then it is unreasonable to expect that they will return next year! Graffiti is a hair-pulling experience for a camp staff. The urban camp in which I am involved "short-circuited" this defacing activity by having a graffiti board, newsprint hung in a common area at our camp's home base, for campers and counselors to leave their names, messages, etc. Also, we had wooden plaques and wood burners available for supervised wood burning. These plaques were treasures that most of our campers took home at the end of the week.

Weapons. (This was a term used by one of our urban campers.) We found, within a couple of days, that a number of the boys had found sticks with pointed ends and kept these as their "weapons." Obviously this was a means of security, and luckily we had no problems. Here is a good reason for trying to create the sense of safety and security during the week, starting with the very first orientation and explanation of rules. As we reinforced the sense of safety and security, the issue of "weapons" decreased.

The final day. We found that having a volunteer photographer along with us during the week, taking slides of everyone and our activities, was a great means of closure. The photographer had the slides developed in time to have a presentation the final evening in the chapel. Everyone saw that they were important in these pictures. It brought the whole week's experience together and was a very positive ending. If the camp staff cannot do this the final evening, then try it within a couple of weeks upon returning home. A promotional event can be planned in the churches, using these slides in the future.

EVALUATION AND REENTRY

Evaluation. Here is where the goal and objectives come in handy again. The director should review the goal and each objective carefully with the steering committee and the counselors. Were the goals and objectives achieved? The answers will provide fodder for developing the next urban camp experience.

Reentry. This is a main reason for the very existence of the urban camp. Reentry is the "planned response after the fact." If the camp is nothing more than a fun experience away from the city, then maybe there is no need for reentry. If the camp experience is designed to further assist the local urban church's religious education work with youth or enhance an after-school or other specialized urban program, then reentry is essential. We in camping ministries can talk about the local church at camp as much as possible, but if the local church is not willing or able to take up where we left off at camp, I am afraid that much of what we achieve at camp is lost once the children return to their urban settings.

Reentry is a well-thought-through response to the experience the children had at camp and a building on that experience. Some urban campers, depending on the camp's objectives and success, will have experienced the "Aha!" of a retreat, sometimes called a "mountain-top experience." Yet, the campers are not generally equipped to interpret or integrate this experience back home. The camp staff, in tandem with the local urban church's religious education staff, should help the former campers integrate the camp experience into their own life in the urban settings, through such things as pointing out that they can become good examples for children their age who were not able to go to camp, or that even in the urban environment one can keep the camp attitudes going—one can be caring and helpful, too. The camp counselors should be utilized in this set of experiences and build on what occurred in the Urban Camp.

Into the City:
The Urban Work Camp

Ron Robotham

Camping is not only an experience where urban children and youth leave the city for an experience in a setting of nature's beauty. Camping can be an experience where those outside of the city come to learn and work in a camping-like program. Urban work projects constitute an exciting possibility for groups seeking service projects that will involve them in significant service to fellow human beings. The benefits of this service work can be many and long lasting.

Much of the dynamics described in the first part of this chapter continues into this new arrangement. Most of the steps of careful planning and preparation and training carry over with only some site specific modifications. Let me add that perspective and open your eyes to this opportunity.

In an urban workcamp the participants risk an encounter with the redemptive power of God-in-the-city. Jesus' call to service included these words, "Bring good news to the poor and proclaim liberty to the captives" (Luke 4:18). Jesus called us as disciples and commissioned us to "go then to all the peoples" (Mathew 28:19) and promised us the power of the Holy Spirit to fill us to "witness for me in Jerusalem, Samaria, and the world" (Acts 1:8). When religious educators follow this call and work for justice, even when sore and tired, Jesus promises that "whenever you do this for one of the least of these brothers and sisters of mine, you do it for me" (Mathew 25:40).

Hear what some participants in urban workcamps have said:

> Our work project in the inner city surprised me. I was not surprised to see the problems, the dirt, the destruction, the pain, or the loss. I was surprised to see so many exciting ministries in progress. Very inspirational to interact with those who live out and act out their faith in such creative ways.

> I've never felt my faith was very real. To act on my faith on a work project has reminded me of *The Velveteen Rabbit* who was "not real until he was loved and worn-out."

When we speak of a work project, a service project, a camp, or an outreach experience we mean much the same thing. A *work project* involves a *group* who *reaches out* to give *time and energy* performing *any task* related to service and *justice* in the world. Here is what that means in greater detail:

A. A group—can be of any size (2-60) but the ideal size is from 6-20. They can be of any age, age spread, or age grouping.

B. Reaching out—we are called by scripture and by the example of Christ. We care, we love, we need to grow outside of our insulated world.

C. Time and energy—to give money is easy. To give sweat, sore muscles, dirty hands, tired feet, hammered thumbs, that is the challenge of God's work.

D. Any task—the needs of God's people are many and varied. Work projects do almost anything needed to serve persons. Construction, cleaning, helping people solve some problems in their lives, learning how the free foodstore works, learning what a social worker really does, sitting in that endless waiting that a bureaucracy requires of the people fighting red tape.

E. Service and justice—no words are stronger or are used more widely through both the Old and New Testaments. We are called to be on the side of "just-ness" (justice) and "rightness" (righteousness).

TWO APPROACHES

People who are interested in urban work projects often are of two different kinds: 1) They may be the urban church thinking of inviting in outside people to help their ministry, or 2) they may be an outside group looking to the city for a growing service experience. Persons who are members of an urban church or agency might be seeking assistance from nonurban sources to help their own ministries in the community or expand their current urban religious education activities. These persons may want to reach out to educate others about urban ministry, witness to their faith/presence in the city, or spiritually share their vision of an urban church with others.

On the other hand, there are nonurban Christians (from the suburbs, a small town, or rural area) who are looking for an urban educational and spiritual growth experience through service. Such individuals may want to help their own denominational mission work or experience a hands-on manifestation of mission. Or such people may be looking for a cross-cultural experience that will help them get a perspective on the hurting world. Or again such persons may seek to experience an active metaphor of the church where they can find Christ at work while they test their own faith and grow in a loving-caring fellowship in a group.

These are good reasons why persons come to the urban arena. Although Christians are called to serve wherever God's people hurt—and that is in the city, the country, on the farm, in the small towns, and anywhere people live—the urban setting has some advantages. In the city we can find new and varied cultural experiences, new and varied racial experiences, and a wealth of choices of ministries with which to work. Urban service projects in which I have worked, taught the Bible, fed the hungry, conducted a neighborhood survey, and worked with youth in recreation, helping the elderly. We have also been involved in urban service work to street people, refugees and homeless people, with substance abuse rehabilitation efforts, and with runaways and throw-aways.

The urban setting often makes it possible to see close up the faith/witness of Christian groups of a different denominational affiliation. We have worked with Protestant evangelicals, main-line Protestant denominations, Roman Catholics of various religious orders, and Jews.

Facilities for religious education and recreation, together with needed services for housing and eating and emergency care, are close at hand. The advantages await the adventurous—and the careful planners.

THE PROCESS—"HOW TO"

Nothing guarantees success like thorough planning. That theme has already been sounded earlier in this chapter. Let me apply it to preparation for the urban workcamp. In this section I highlight some of the overlooked details, some of the common mistakes, and some common do's and don'ts. We all plan for the obvious, like "how do we get there." But what about the not so obvious. When the host church says "kitchen available," does that mean they have a pot big enough to make sloppy joes for forty people? Or ovens large and hot enough to bake lasagna? Or a refrigerator to hold gallons of milk?

We hope to learn from the mistakes of others. We have made many of our own mistakes, and we have seen mistakes of others. We encourage urban religious educators to talk to those who have done such projects before. Urban religious educators should especially try to talk to a group who may have gone to the specific setting in which they are going. The church or agency in which an urban religious educator is working should be able to provide the names of other help for contact persons.

The following is a list of some of the most important practical points which my colleagues and I have learned about effectively conducting an urban camp.

I. PLANNING—THE GIVENS

First, intentionality is crucial. Deciding to go on a work project is an exciting, scary decision. When a group first asks, "Where do we start?" I answer, "What are your parameters? What factors do you need or want in a work project?" They usually answer, "What are you talking about?"

We all have some "givens" in which our decisions are made. Maybe its money. Maybe a person can only go a hundred miles from home. Maybe a person is looking for a certain type of experience. Maybe a certain ethnic group experience is wanted. Sort out the givens under these headings:

A. Type of work project—with senior citizens? families? churches?

B. Type of work—rehabilitation, recreation, teaching, construction, agriculture, day care, Bible school?

C. Type of organization—organize your own, use established project, in-between?

D. Limits in the group—time of year available, length of time, age of participants, skill level, campers?

E. Details—How far? How much money? Accommodation needs, traditions within your group, type of transportation?

II. PLANNING THE DETAILS

Know who does what. In a work project there are many details to be worked out. The religious educator does not have to do them all personally, but somebody does. Knowing who does what means assignments to groups and individuals. The groups involved are usually the participants—the sponsoring group—the host group.

III. PLANNING—SOME REMINDERS

• *Permission slip*—Have the parent's insurance company and policy number. Check on shots, expecially tetanus. Some groups automatically have everyone get one before they go, just in case.

• *Clothing lists*—Everyone wears tennis shoes these days! Encourage hard-soled shoes.

• *Food*—How many burners on the stove? How big an oven? How many pans? Pots? Utensils? Spatulas? Carrot peelers? Paring knives? Refrigeration? Enough for ten gallons of milk? Any freezer space? Know the facility and plan accordingly.

• *Parking*—Think ahead. The big church bus may not be able to be parked in the inner city. Fancy motorhomes may not be an appropriate witness to the work project presence.

• *Showers*—Make sure there are showers somewhere! Set up access through some school, recreation center, or gym.

- *Extras*—Where to get an ice cream treat? a cold pop?
- *Supplies* for the project (paint, hardware, tools). Where to get more?
- *Bank accounts* and *charge accounts*—Do they need to be set up ahead of time?
- *First Aid*—Closest hospital? Doctor available? First-aid kits in every work crew?

IV. PLANNING THE ORGANIZATION

Dividing the group into work teams beforehand and appointing team leaders avoids on-site hassles. Know who is "in charge" of the group. Be sure the adults have worked this all out before coming on site. Know who gives directions on each work crew. If the religious educator is in a project with several groups, he or she should make time for each group to be together for sharing and clearing the air.

Get the group away off site once in a while. Some city projects for example are intense in interaction with needy children hungry for love. That is very tiring. It is an important part of religious education work in the city, but you need get away to recharge occasionally.

Groups ask, "What do you see as the biggest problems most often neglected by work groups?"

First is orientation. A) Groupness—both leaders and all participants should be prepared intentionally. Get close as a group; know each other. Know who's in charge. B) Education—know where you are going. Be educated. Know the people you work with; know the history of the people. Know the background of the work the agency is doing and has done. C) Spiritual preparation—you are called by God into religious education work. You go as the very hands and feet of God to do this work. Study and pray. Have a scriptural basis for your work. Know why you go and in whose name you serve.

Second is credibility. Some workcamp participants expect to go off and save the world. But the participants are the servants; they are the outsiders. They go to be taught and to learn. Urban religious education workers must earn their credibility by treating trust and openness as sacred and by being God's humble servants.

Third is assumptions. *Don't assume!* Know. Know who does

what. Ask a million questions. Get answers. Letters may work; phone calls are better, but nothing can replace the on-site visit before the project starts.

This kind of camping, going into the city, and the kind we think of more commonly, leaving the city to go to the camp, are similar intense experiences that change lives. Small groups of people live together in a way that brings them to a new depth of appreciation of both the tasks and the victories of Christian living.

Chapter 16

Other Models for Urban Church Education (Briefly Noted)

Donald B. Rogers

In exploring programs in urban church education to be described in this book I became acquainted with some efforts that should be mentioned even though, for various reasons, a full description is not possible. I am listing those in this section as "briefly noted" in the hope that they too will provide stimulus for creative adaptation by those experimenting and exploring in this ministry.

A NEIGHBORHOOD CLUB MODEL

I became aware of a neighborhood club model in a midwestern city that features a very strong commitment by the leaders. One basic principle is to do those things that allow for full identification with children and youth. It is almost a surrogate parent relationship model.

This means that the staff are full-time, live in the neighborhoods in which they serve, and make at least a five-year commitment to urban religious education. One leader commented that what these city kids do not need is someone else to appear and soon disappear from their lives. They need some continuity of adult presence. Thus the "round-the-clock" availability made possible by living near-by, and the promise of "I'll be here" that comes from the five-year commitment have been held to with tenacity.

The formal parts of the program are built in response to the needs that are identified in the relationships. Leaders are encouraged to limit the number of children they work with in order to allow depth to develop in the relationships. If the appropriate formal program is an after-school Bible study, then this kind of religious education program is developed. If it is a self-esteem project involving grooming and clothing, that is the direction taken. If mothers want to get involved, a mother's club is begun.

It was this group that pointed out how critical the concept of turf is in some urban situations. They discovered that it was usually better to take children on day camping expeditions by recognized turf divisions than to mix groups across those established lines.

A STORE-FRONT SANCTUARY MODEL

Another program I learned about is a store-front after-school program for grade-school children in urban settings. What I found unique was a concept of sanctuary that guided the program. Children were welcomed into the program on the basis of their desire to participate. It was an "open door" program. But the participation was on the leader's terms of rules for behavior. These included respect for property, the exclusion of some kinds of "street" language (a matter of vocabulary *and* style), cooperation with group activities and decisions, and other things like that.

But this leader made it a point to distinguish for the children the difference between what was expected in this "sanctuary" and what was necessary sometimes on the street. She knew that survival on the street or around the neighborhood required some patterns of behavior that some people might not think were "nice." Nice or not, they were necessary, and she did not want to send children out to be hurt because of a vulnerability she had encouraged that was beyond their years.

"In here we behave this way because this is a sanctuary. Out there you may have to look out for yourself and behave differently, and I understand." She said that the children understood too and were able to live with that realization about different places and different behaviors.

COMPUTERS AND URBAN CHURCH EDUCATION

There is not much mention in this book of computers as part of the opportunity in urban religious education. The fact is, however, that the PC is becoming a common electronic aid in all kinds of religious education. Some churches have found willing sponsors in their own or other congregations—sometimes through businesses and foundations—to make the computers and the software programs available. It seems to be a "fundable" resource.

The computers are being used to do after-school tutoring. They are being made the focal point of summer programs—like a form of Vacation Church School or a camping program. The children are becoming computer literate in their public school classrooms and homes and find the computer a comfortable teacher. Kenneth Bedell has written on this subject in a helpful manner.[1] More useful and affordable software is becoming available rapidly.

Computers can be impressively patient and positive so that the individualization of education assistance fits this electronic capability very well. The software can sometimes solve a leader's problem (we do not know how to give them the tutoring assistance in what they need to know, new math for example, but the software is available). Coordination with the neighborhood public school is often the key to getting good general education software references. Denominational publishing houses, religious bookstores, and some mail order houses have the key to religious education software.

One summer program is able to successfully combine an intense computer-based remedial program with a residential camp experience. The camp is the climax that keeps some kids working at the remedial effort. If they particpate in the remedial program with sufficient regularity then they are invited to attend the camp as the final week of the program.

EDUCATING THE WHOLE CONGREGATION
TO MISSION

A major dimension of urban church education is implied by some of our authors as they describe the place and role of the urban church in general, educating a whole urban congregation to the vision and means of church service.

Chris Michael has done some excellent work in this area with her denomination, the Church of the Brethren, and has shared her insights in a seminar in 1988, in Chicago (SCUPE). Here is a brief outline of the major points of her presentation:

Congregations need to learn these things in order to come alive to an urban ministry:

A. Recognize the biblical and theological resources, the history of the church as an urban reality—all this undergirds, as appropriate, religious education in cities.

B. Use sociological information—it helps church people get a clear grasp of the dynamics of urban life.

C. Be conscious of the transient nature of urban populations.

D. Learn the dimensions of pluralism.

E. Know the human needs that are "on the doorstep" of every urban church.

F. Sense the intense need people have for community.

G. Learn that urban neighborhoods often relate on the basis of chosen (secondary) relationships, while people in some other contexts relate on the basis of expected (primary) relationships.

H. Learn how to decipher the systems and the operation of those systems of urban life—beyond the individual, beyond the neighborhood.

She went on to list some strategic principles of effectiveness that, in a sense, become the curriculum and the method of learning to be effective in urban church ministry.

1. Learn how to listen.
2. Visit your church neighbors.
3. Seek out and pay attention to the people in other churches, in businesses, in schools of a neighborhood.
4. Invite the people of the neighborhood and city to come and tell you their stories.

5. Be active in all community associations and organizations.
6. Study the census data.
7. Work ecumenically.
8. Learn how to give *and receive* in mutual ministry.
9. Build partnerships with other organizations to do ministry, solve problems, work on issues.
10. Genuinely *receive* new people—until they really belong.
11. Respond to *felt* needs, not what you think their needs ought to be.
12. Do not be content with dealing with symptoms of ills, go to the root causes in "public ministry."
13. Share your resources, share your experience—the successes and the failures.
14. Know that the dailyness of life is most often where the gospel becomes incarnate.
15. Take risks.
16. Balance nurture of people (and self) with outreach.[2]

EDUCATING FOR ECONOMIC AWARENESS

William Granville Jr. has established an interesting experiment in urban religious education with church sponsorship in New Jersey—Trenton and Princeton being two of the sites. His goal is to help in the economic integration of blacks into America. To reach this goal he has designed an academy in which selected black youth are helped to become familiar with the workings of the business and financial life of America, the fundamentals of the free enterprise system. Businessmen and ministers have become a part of this process.

Youth are nominated by their pastors for the program on the basis of the interest and potential that is seen. They attend intensive seminars and are involved in summer internship programs that depend on area business people for implementation. Participants not only learn about financial and business programs from the people who lead them, they are also helped to develop the motivation and social and interpersonal skills needed if the goal of economic integration is to be reached.

The program is noteworthy as a model of how one who made it into an arena of life turns around to help others along the same path. William Granville is an executive of the Mobil Oil Company in New Jersey.

FROM LITERACY TO A COLLEGE DEGREE

The joining together of a Roman Catholic university and a parish is yet another viable model of urban religious education. The parish sits in a neighborhood of low educational achievement. Many people are functionally illiterate. Teaching them how to read is a major educational objective. But that is just the beginning. The commitment of the university (staff and students) is that they will work with anyone with the ability and willingness to make it all the way through to a college degree.

Learning how to read is a first step in a journey that is presented to the "beginners" as a possible dream. Literacy is followed by tutoring, by preparation for the GED, by job and career counseling, by placement assistance, by college acceptance and tutoring as needed to, as far as possible, surround the participant from beginning to end in an atmosphere of success.

The long-term commitment to individuals addresses a major learning problem, that of low self-esteem and low personal confidence.

The parish parochial school, the CCD programs, the literacy for adults program, the after-school tutoring, the neighborhood public school are all seen as vital parts of a holistic plan of making a long term impact on the total educational needs of a particular group of people. The focus and limitation are part of the model that make it work.

THE FULL CURRICULUM ACADEMY/COLLEGE

Full-blown academy/college models of adult religious education have been developed in a variety of places. The intent in these is to help individual churches do what they could not do on their own, that is, provide serious credentialing and accredited adult religious education for those who wish to engage in such a process.

The Fellowship Bible Institute of San Francisco is one such program. With a focus on preparing men and women for Christian leadership, the Institute makes it possible for those who are somewhere along the line of educational progress from an incomplete high-school education and beyond to enter programs that address their needs and interests.

Formal admission procedures, counseling in educational goal setting, enrollment in an appropriate curriculum, instruction, testing, and fulfillment of requirements for completion constitute the format on a variety of differing tracks. Classes meet in both the afternoon and evening hours. A General Certificate program is available for those who did not finish high school or are interested in a self-enrichment process. Full completion of the course of studies in the GC involves successful work in thirty to fifty courses. A Certificate in Advanced Christian Studies is available, at the college level, but not for college credit. This is a one-year study program of six courses selected from nine areas. The Institute also offers Associate of Arts programs at an accredited college level on two tracks, one in biblical studies and the other in biblical studies plus a ministerial major. These program are approximately four to five years in length. Fees are kept at a minimum to encourage broad participation, but standards are kept high.

The program shows the creative initiative of Dessie Webster (Founder), Stanley B. Long (President), and Mark Lou Branson (Dean). Alongside the Institute are a variety of supportive programs including a preparatory school, a pre-school, a counseling center, and various community service projects. The intent is that the wholeness of ministry would be present in and around the academic process. Fellowship Urban Outreach is the umbrella organization for the entire scope of programs.

THE MULTICULTURAL RELIGIOUS EDUCATION MODEL

I have included here a more extended statement of some work that has been done in respect to churches that do not fit within the major population of the white church. These are churches that serve more than one cultural constituency. These are churches that have teachers from one culture and students from another and find themselves with educational problems of a perplexing nature.

It has been noted elsewhere in this book that one of the problems most often mentioned is that of curriculum resources. Until fairly recently the assumed setting for many curriculum items was white, middle-class, suburban or rural American. To some extent that slant continues.

The result is that many urban religious educators both voice and hear the statement, "My students can't find themselves in these materials." Changes in the color of the people in the pictures, translation of the materials into some other language than standard English, some changes of the configuration of family patterns are inadequate though welcomed attempts to increase the pluralism of the resources.

A major issue in curriculum resource production for all the producers is the economic issue. Most publishing houses, church-related or not, have to pay their own way, thus have to calculate materials production on the basis of sales, and thus have a hard time serving small markets.

The issue of resource pluralism is complicated by the varieties of goals in the churches. One set of materials prepared by black Protestants for black Protestants was judged in one curriculum review session as being "too black." The black teachers indicated that they wanted to have their children grow into an acceptance of other children and did not want an all black image in the resources. Others, of course, want the resources to fully focus on black identity.

A further complication arises when some of the most pressing social issues which religious education might address are so sensitive that publishers refrain from addressing them. The fear is that a move toward relevancy will be interpreted as prejudice.

Various ethnic groups find a similar lack of consensus on the role of religious education. Some want the church education experience to be a major teacher of national, cultural, ethnic identity. Religious education programs are to include native language instruction, the history of the "mother" country, and cultural values and practices as well as Christianity. For some, that is. Others want the religious education programs to help their children to become enculturated in the American patterns. The resource publisher finds no clear mandate in an already small marketing situation.

The answer seems to be in a combination of efforts. One: Publishers should be encouraged to work toward inclusiveness in a pluralistic arena. That is, the major thrust of the materials should be as inclusive as possible. Two: Publishers should be encouraged to publish supplementary materials on a cost or even a loss basis to help fill the gaps between the main line of materials and various ethnic and racial groups. Cooperative efforts across denominational lines could help to take the editorial and financial burden off any one publisher. Three: Local religious educators should be provided with special training opportunities in resource modification—how to re-edit, supplement, write new materials, and modify for local usage. Four: Churches should begin to share their efforts more freely. I have found that churches that do what is suggested in step three above are reluctant to share their work with others. I know the reasons are a mixture of uneasiness about the quality of the work done, a desire to maintain control of the work, and an uncertainty about the reception of their work by others. The unfortunate aspect is that unnecessary duplication of effort and lack of encouragement is the result. Five: Publishers need to realize that urbanization as such is *the* dominant trend in the population shifts in the world. The whole world is being urbanized and the church in all lands, all ethnic arenas, all nationalities already needs the materials that are not yet available. The market of the future for materials should be a world market and increasingly culturally relevant. Six: Publishers and local church educators should recognize that resource materials preparation is enhanced by a "from the ground up" approach where the "consumers" of the materials are the creators of the materials.

Smaller churches that become integrated find themselves in a peculiar situation of teacher-pupil difference. The neighborhood, let us say, as seems to be a recent pattern, has changed from white to black. The church has remained and is still mostly white in its adult population, but a group of neighborhood black children come to the Vacation Bible School and then enroll in Sunday morning church school. White teachers, often it seems in their older years, now have black children as students. The desire to be good teachers is intense, but goodwill is not enough.

The teachers have a limited awareness of differences. Their

experience and training seem only partially relevant. As of yet their contacts with the parents of the children are limited. They feel inadequate and frustrated.

Letty Russell addresses this issue in her article with the suggestion that part of the answer is to "indigenize" the teaching staff as rapidly as possible and to rethink the characteristics of the "desirable teacher" to be more inclusive. Another step could be, should be, training experiences that will help the available teachers reach the understandings of cultural differences that they need.

Marina Herrera has prepared a very useful analysis of the Hispanic adult learner for the training of religious education personnel. It is a model of what is needed. She writes this summary of the situation:

"The methods used in the religious education for Hispanics should keep these specific characteristics of the adult Hispanic learner in mind:

"First. The experiences that Hispanics bring to the learning process should be given the prominence they deserve. These experiences include, among others: the hardships of immigration, political persecution, material privation, unjust imprisonment, linguistic isolation, racial discrimination, feelings of failure. Among the positives: the quest for justice and freedom, desire to give one's children a better life, perseverance in the faith in spite of all obstacles, the deep sense of the sacredness of life and of God's providential care, human warmth, and joy.

"Second. The tendency is to see culture as static and not as a dynamic reality that can be changed and should be changed, altered, or adapted to meet the demands of the gospel and of the historic moment in which we find ourselves. Those methods, then, that encourage cultural and social analysis are to be preferred to those that consider religious education as a process of spiritualization without incarnation as a concrete and sometimes harsh reality of the present. The use of such analysis should enable Hispanics to see themselves as both creator and creature of culture and of social and family structures.

"Third. The Hispanic cultural preference for the three-dimensional spoken word over the one-dimensional printed word demands that the methods used in the religious education of Hispanics rely heavily on the personal, direct exchanges between the teacher and the student. Teachers will need to be persons of creativity who are willing to seek other than the traditional ways of communication in order to get their message across.

"Fourth. The flexibility of the attitude of the Hispanics to time, and their relative attachment to place, point to the need for flexible schedules and physical arrangements for carrying out successful learning experiences. Teachers working with Hispanics need to be people who are capable of making adjustments to schedules and to accommodate themselves in less than optimal surroundings for the sake of making the teaching/learning encounter more accessible. Instead of having the people come to the teacher, it is necessary to bring the teaching to them.

"Fifth. To suggest or devise criteria for the evaluation of religious education programs for Hispanics may be premature at this stage in our awareness of the distinct character of Hispanic religious education."[3]

The complexity of the issues in multicultural religious education is indicated by Herrera's helpful use of the concept of context in communication. Working with the research of Edward Hall she writes,

"Hall suggests that cultures can be grouped based on the way in which they use verbal communication. He finds two basic styles and places the cultures on an axis between these two depending on how far or how close they are to his description of these two styles:

L	Swiss-Germans
O	Germans
W	Scandinavians
	White U.S.
	French
	English
	Italians
H	[Black U.S.] Herrera's addition
I	Spanish
G	Greeks
H	Arabs

"In low context cultures verbal instructions must be able to stand on their own; i.e., not be dependent on context. In high context cultures verbal instructions depend more on context situations and feelings than on the words used. So if a teacher of religion from a low context culture is trying to communicate with a person from a high context culture but does not accompany the words with the emotional and contextual nonverbal communication which the hearer is accustomed to, the communication exchange will be very poor. The high context person will not respond in the way the communicator expects and tensions and frustrations will be the result. When high context people try to communicate with low context ones, the high degree of nonverbal elements they use serve as static in the communication process and the low context person cannot "hear" above the facial expressions and body movements that fill the communication style of high context persons."[4]

There is much work yet to be done before works like that of Marina Herrera are available for the many groups and age levels where they are needed. What do we do in the meantime?

I suggest that the interim strategies be based on a twofold recognition that cultural differences are of great significance in religious education and that learning is learning in a generic form across all lines of individuality as well as culture. Both truths, held in tension, will prevent us from ignoring the problems with facile stereotyping of any of the participants and help us to avoid the sense of despair and rapid burnout that can arise from frustration.

With that polar affirmation in mind we can consciously reduce the teacher-student ratio to make individualization of attention possible. Realism about the ratio at the beginning can help to provide the constructive context where problems can be resolved, learnings take place, and skills improved. Then the classes and programs can be enlarged.

Also we can be more open and frank in our teacher training discussions without fear of offense. If the agenda is not "right or wrong" but frankly exploratory, and if the attitude is one of helpfulness and the goal mutual growth, then teachers can help each other become increasingly more effective. This suggests that many of the most valid insights into multicultural religious education are apt to arise out of the thoughtful experience of the practitioners.

Whether the situation is one of homogeneity or heterogeneity of race, culture, ethnic orientation, national origin; whether the issues are of those of culture or language; whatever the character of the pluralism or majority/minority status, the history of the movement of the faith across many lines in the past indicates that the problems can be overcome.

Notes

1. Kenneth Bedell, *The Role of Computers in Religious Education* (Valley Forge, Pa.: Judson Press, 198?)

2. These are part of the Education for Urban Ministry (EFUM) program of the Church of the Brethren. Chris Michaels is the director of that program.

3. Marina Herrera, *Adult Religious Education for the Hispanic Community* (Washington, D.C.: National Conference of Diocesan Directors of Religious Education, 1988), pp. 55, 56. In the original document the terms "catechetics" and "catechesis" were used where we have inserted "religious education" and "teacher."

4. Ibid., p. 30. See also E. Hall, *The Silent Language* (Garden City, Anchor, 1963) and E. Hall, *The Hidden Dimension* (Garden City: Doubleday, 1966).

Appendix I

Results of the
URBAN MINISTRIES RELIGIOUS
EDUCATION NEEDS ASSESSMENT

Colleen Birchett

(*EDITOR'S NOTE: In her chapter on the history of religious education in the black church, Colleen Birchett identifies a personally conducted research program on recognized needs. She uses that material in her chapter in summary form. The fuller statement is included here.*)

In 1986 the staff and volunteers of Urban Ministries began a formal needs assessment in black churches in Chicago. Under the direction of Colleen Birchett, 200 members of local churches, including 60 Sunday school superintendents, about 60 pastors and about 70 members of the following church programs and auxiliaries met for brainstorming these categories: 1) Evangelism and Outreach, 2) Worship Service Auxiliaries, 3) Religious Education, 4) Ministries to Black Women, 5) Ministries to Black Men, 6) Ministries to Youth, 7) Deacons and Trustees.

The participants were asked the following questions:

a) What are the primary missions of the black church?
b) What are the most important programs and auxiliaries used to achieve the mission of the black church?
c) How do the missions of each of these programs and auxiliaries relate to the mission of the black church?
d) What are the most important activities of these programs and auxiliaries?
e) What skills are needed by members of these programs and auxiliaries in carrying out the mission(s) of the black church?

Answers received from the various groups of participants were then condensed, and an 8-page questionnaire was developed. This questionnaire was then distributed to 4,000 black churches nationwide. Of the black churches surveyed, 220 completed the questionnaire—a 6% response rate. This is a higher response rate than was gotten by a similar study by Scripture Press in 1970 (3.8% response rate) but lower than the response rate for Leland (1986), whose response was 66 completed questionnaires out of 347 distributed (18% response rate).

The Results

Here is a summary of the results of the Urban Ministries Needs Assessment.

What is the most important mission of the black church?

		Rank
1)	to worship God together as a people	1.7
2)	to evangelize lost blacks	2.7
3)	to educate black people	4.2
4)	to heal personal and family problems	4.2
5)	to develop black leadership	4.6
6)	to improve communications between blacks	6.2
7)	to promote racial pride and confidence	6.4
8)	to provide social services	6.8
9)	to organize for political action	8.3

What programs and auxiliary areas are most important for achieving the mission of the black church?

		Rank
1)	Evangelism/Outreach	2.5
2)	Religious Education	3.0
3)	Worship Service Auxiliaries	4.6
4)	Ministries to Youth	4.8
5)	Deacon Board	4.9
6)	Trustees	5.4
7)	Ministries to Black Men	5.42
8)	Ministries to Black Women	5.8
9)	Fundraising	7.9

What programs and auxiliaries are the most in need of training?

		Rank
1)	Evangelism/Outreach	2.6
2)	Religious Education	2.9
3)	Ministries to Youth	4.7
4)	Deacon Board	5.02
5)	Worship Service Auxiliaries	5.04
6)	Ministries to Black Men	5.3
7)	Trustees	5.36

8) Ministries to Black Women   5.7
9) Fundraising   7.9

In what areas do people involved in Evangelism need training?

		Rank
1)	Selecting Scriptures for Needs	3.15
2)	Developing Evangelistic Tutorials	3.96
3)	Analyzing the Community Surrounding Church	4.42
4)	House to House Visitation	4.47
5)	Appealing to Gang Members	6.07
6)	Crusades and Street Meetings	6.24
7)	Assisting Drug Addicts	6.3
8)	Reaching Seniors	6.66
9)	Locating Black-Oriented Gospel Tracts	6.87
10)	Relating to Pimps and Prostitutes	6.96

In what areas do Church Christian Education Leaders need training?

		Rank
1)	Teaching Scriptural Principles	1.6
2)	Training for Service in the Church	2.2
3)	Training for Service outside the Church	3.5
4)	Promoting memory of Bible Passages	4.5
5)	Teaching Black History and Culture	5.2
6)	Training Nonmembers	6.0
7)	Teaching Psychological Principles	6.3
8)	Raising Level of Political Awareness	6.5

In what areas do Sunday School Superintendents need training?

		Rank
1)	Recruiting and Training Teachers	1.8
2)	Involving Parents	4.3
3)	Developing Youth Leadership	4.85
4)	Evangelistic Strategies	4.88
5)	Handling Staff Personalities	5.4
6)	Designing Devotionals for Children	5.6
7)	Getting Pastoral Involvement	6.13
8)	Managing Sunday School Time	6.15
9)	Preserving Black History and Culture	7.9
10)	Keeping Sunday School Records	8.0

What training is most badly needed by persons working in ministries to youth?

		Rank
1)	Teaching Youth the Bible	2.6
2)	Evangelizing lost Black Youth	3.2
3)	Involving Youth in the Worship Service	4.0
4)	Counseling Youth	4.9

5) Developing Youth Fellowships   5.4
6) Sex Education and/or Pregnancy Counseling   6.8
7) Basic Education Skills   7.0
8) Teaching Black History and Culture   7.6
9) Presenting Alternatives to Gangs   7.8
10) Teaching Youth Vocational Skills   8.1
11) Ministering to Detained Youth   8.8

What training is most badly needed by Deacons?

	Rank
1) Teaching	2.6
2) Evangelizing	3.5
3) Assisting with the Worship Service	3.9
4) Caring for Members	4.7
5) Organizing Fellowships	6.1
6) Solving Community Problems	6.3
7) Caring for the Pastor	6.5
8) Maintaining the Church Building	7.8
9) Working with Community Agencies	8.4
10) Keeping Church Records	8.9

What training is most badly needed by Persons in Various Worship Auxiliaries?

	Rank
1) Detecting Spiritual Needs of People	2.2
2) Bringing Congregation to One Accord	2.5
3) Conducting Prayer Meetings	3.8
4) Selecting Scripture Readings	4.1
5) Selecting Music for Special Needs	4.9
6) Conducting Testimonial Services	5.4
7) Vocal Performance	6.559
8) Administering Special Sacraments	6.559

What training is most badly needed by Persons Involved in Ministering to Black Men?

	Rank
1) Teaching Biblical Principles of Family Life	2.6
2) Developing Male Leaders for the Church	3.7
3) Developing Male Leaders for the Community	4.3
4) Showing Christianity is not Effeminate	5.1
5) Helping Old and Young Men to Communicate	5.6
6) Developing All-Male Bible Studies	6.5
7) Ministering in Prisons	7.3
8) Developing Male Vocational Skills	7.9
9) Developing All-Male Socials	8.7
10) Developing All-Male Athletic Activities	9.3

What training is most badly needed by Persons Involved in Ministering to Black Women?

		Rank
1)	Teaching Biblical Principles of Family Life	2.6
2)	Evangelizing Black Women	3.2
3)	Counseling Black Women	3.9
4)	Developing Black Female Leaders	4.3
5)	Helping Old and Young Women to Communicate	4.9
6)	Developing All-Female Bible Studies	5.7
7)	Developing Female Vocational Skills	6.7
8)	Ministering to Female Prisoners	6.9
9)	Developing All-Female Socials	7.8
10)	Developing All-Female Athletic Activities	8.8

Appendix II

List of the Issues in Urban Religious Education Survey of United Methodists

Donald B. Rogers

EDITOR'S NOTE: This is a full list of the responses of the graduates of United Seminary who participated in the survey on urban religious education needs conducted by Donald B. Rogers and mentioned in chapter one.

HIGH PRIORITY ITEMS FROM SURVEY

Ways to do community surveys
Social remedial programs
Age level groupings
Racism
Organizational issues
Lesson preparation
Video presentations
Financing issues

SECONDARY PRIORITY ITEMS FROM SURVEY

How to find relevant curriculum resources
How to create relevant curriculum resources
Special interest groupings
Literacy programs
Behavioral issues
Discipline
When parents aren't involved

Senior citizen classes
Drama skills
Cooperation with other churches

LOW PRIORITY ITEMS FROM SURVEY
PLUS
ADDITIONAL ITEMS MENTIONED BY RESPONDENTS

Ways to determine leadership potential
After school club formats
Camping, retreat, workcamp formats
Literacy programs
Drug abuse
Sex education
Work skills
Teacher recruitment
Teacher education
Storytelling
Bible study
Cooperation with other churches in the neighborhood
Education as evangelism
Education of shut-ins
Teacher appreciation
Teacher burn-out
Enlisting volunteers
Influencing community organizations
Career counseling (including job hunting skills)
Christian education and church growth
Christian education and outreach
Chrysalis community
Budgeting (family)
Clown ministry
Puppet ministry
Organized community action groups
Remedial education
Recreation
Young adults ministry
Child abuse
Spouse abuse
Parent-teen relationships
Lay counseling
Co-op child care
Latch key education
Legal rights
Family structures and life

Utilizing comm. resources
Grant writing
Licensing procedures
Self-defense
Teen pregnancy
Values - morals
Conflict management
Listening skills
Crafts
Role models
Devotional skills
Many-aged classes
Evaluation of programs
Self-esteem
Neighboring
Unemployment
Scouts
4-H
Healing
Education through worship
Basics

Profiles of Contributors

(listed in the order of their contribution)

EDITOR'S NOTE: Because this volume seeks to incorporate the theories and practices of a wide number of Christian confessions, the contributors are representative of a wide spectrum of Christian religious educators including Catholics, mainline Protestants, and evangelical Protestants. In addition to the Catholic contributor, authors in this volume come from the following Protestant denominations (in alphabetical order): African Methodist Episcopal Zion, American Baptist, Church of the Brethren, Presbyterian (USA), Southern Baptist, United Church of Christ, and United Methodist.

DONALD B. ROGERS a native of Cincinnati, is Professor of Religious Education at United Seminary in Dayton. He also serves as pastor of the urban Mt. Auburn Baptist Church. His books include *In Praise of Learning, The Way of the Teacher,* and *Teachable Moments.* His involvement in urban religious education extends over his entire career, and he has served in this capacity in Baptist, Christian Church (Disciples), and Presbyterian congregations.

LETTY RUSSELL, from Connecticut, is Professor of Theology at Yale University Divinity School. Her books include *Christian Education in Mission, Growth in Partnership,* and *Household of*

Freedom. Early in her career she worked in an East Harlem church.

CHRIS MICHAEL, from Elgin Illinois, directs the Education for Urban Ministry Program (EFUM) of congregational renewal for urban Church of the Brethren congregations. She has served as a pastor in an urban parish in Indianapolis.

KAY KUPPER BERG from Dayton, Ohio, is on the faculty of the English Department of Sinclair Community College in that city. She also is a religious education leader in her urban church. She has served as chairwoman of a Curriculum Coordinating Committee that has designed and implemented a core religious education curriculum for grades 7-12. She is the co-author of a book of pedagogical vignettes, *Teachable Moments.*

C. RENEE RUST has served as resident coordinator of Studies in Spirituality in the dioceses of Covington and Cincinnati. Her D. Min. is from United Theological Seminary. Among her publications is the book *Making the Psalms Your Prayer.* She is past presider of the College Theology Society's national section on Sacramental Life and Liturgy Task Force.

COLLEEN BIRCHETT is Curriculum Specialist for a consortium of Chicago colleges and also serves as editor of *Inteen* magazine for black youth published by Urban Ministries. Additionally, she conducts workshops designed to improve religious education in black churches. Her doctorate is from the University of Michigan. She is the author of *Christian Education and the Mission of the Black Church.*

ROBERT E. JONES, from Dayton, Ohio, is adjunct faculty member of United Seminary and co-pastor of the College Hill Community Church. His doctorate is from Yale University Divinity School, where he later became Assistant Professor of Practical Theology. He has held many positions on urban committees and task forces around the country, and is an officer of the National Black Child Development Institute.

CAPTOLIA D. NEWBERN, from Philadelphia, holds six university and seminary degrees including an Ed.D. from Columbia University and a D.Min. from United Seminary, the latter earned when she was eighty years old. She has taught at seven different institutions of higher learning, and is currently on the leadership team in the AMEZ-CME Commission on Union. Her publications include books on stewardship, reconciliation, missionary organization, and the black family.

LAWRENCE L. FALK, from Minnesota, is Professor of Sociology and Chairman of the Department of Sociology and Social Work at Concordia College. His doctorate came from the University of Nebraska. He has published widely and is active as a consultant.

WILLIAM R. MYERS of Chicago is Associate Professor of Religious Education and Director of the D.Min. program at Chicago Theological Seminary. His doctorate was gained at Loyola University of Chicago, and he has published a book entitled *Theological Themes of Youth Ministry*. Among his many activities is the clinical supervision of seminarians at Chicago's Urban Academy which he himself helped develop.

BILL GAMBRELL, from Jackson, Mississippi, has degrees from the University of Louisville and Southwestern Baptist Theological Seminary. He has conducted numerous workshops in church growth for pastors, religious educators, and adult program leaders.

TOM BOOMERSHINE is Professor of New Testament at United Theological Seminary. His doctorate is from Union Theological Seminary in New York. He is the author of *Story Journey: An Invitation to the Gospel as Storytelling*. The founder of the Network of Biblical Storytellers, he has also produced a series of videotapes *The Victory of Jesus*. He has served inner city churches in East Harlem and East New York, as well as in the West Side of Chicago.

TERRY HECK, from Lancaster, Ohio, was the founding president of the National Association of Released Time Christian Education. She is on the staff of the Council of Christian Communions in Cincinnati, concentrating on the Council's programs for released time.

NELLIE METZ of Kettering, Ohio, taught for thirty-two years in the Ohio public schools, and later served as the religious education director of her church where she developed an innovative supplementary Christian school model.

RICHARD L. STACKPOLE, from Odessa, N.Y., is pastor of a parish in that city. A holder of a degree from United Theological Seminary, he had years of inner-city experience as a social worker in the midwest before developing the first Urban Ministries Camp for the Central New York Conference of his denomination.

RON ROBOTHAM of Michigan has had a wide variety of educational experience including teaching camp administration at United Theological Seminary, twenty-one years of work as a camp manager and leader, and eighteen years of teaching in the public schools. His experience also includes housing project habilitation work through Habitat for Humanity in urban and rural settings.

Index of Names

Index of Subjects

209

and Roman Catholics 156
leadership 152
legality 154, 160
Wilberforce University 78
Worship
  and inclusive church 98
  and religious education 132
  as test of the church 105

Yokefellow Institute 67, 70
YMCA 78
YWCA 78
Youth ministry 127f
  and worship 130
  Bible study 58, 59
  closed circle model 128
  cross generational 132
  pyramid model 127